NEMO

Thomas Cole, *Italian Coast Scene with Ruined Tower*
(1838)

NEMO

X

gnOme

gnOme books
gnomebooks.wordpress.com

Please address inquiries to:
gnomebooks@gmail.com

ISBN-13: 978-0692124444
ISBN-10: 0692124446

Cover image source:

https://upload.wikimedia.org/wikipedia/commons/9
/9b/Italian_Coast_Scene_with_Ruined_Tower-
1838-Thomas_Cole.jpg

Si nemo ex me quærat, scio.
– Augustine of Hippo, *Confessions*

We merrily sing the song of hopelessness.
– *Song of the New Life*

. . . vo significando.
– Dante, *Purgatorio*

The dream happens, nothing does | A seed in me grows | Your whole world is my belly | My name no one knows.

Have nothing to say or feel | Have nothing to do | Have everything that is real | Have none besides who.

Empty mine, abandoned me | A whirlwind of dust | Water flowing to the sea | Between love and lust.

Doesn't matter, don't matter | You say, say, and say | What never was, I chatter | Will never away.

During the storm, in the dark | Only black to see | These blind eyes embrace a spark | Neither you nor me.

The beloved—never wrong | For always to love | Is the harsh command a song | Its absence a dove.

Atom outside time and space | Tiny all of life | Unseen by the human race | Devoid of our strife.

A whole cosmos came and went | Still the I remained | Time into zero bent | Whereon me is chained.

Losing all by losing naught | Floating on a sigh | In a net of falling caught | Flying up to die.

Secretly in secret think | Hiddenly in love | Safestly in safety drink | This fire from above.

Talk to me until I die | Now in pure silence | This tear's whisper is the cry | Of your defiance.

Waiting on a spiral word | Never not to come | Trailing for forever's bird | A line and a crumb.

To gut thyself for nothing | And let loose a sun | To bleed everything | And get through to none.

Hollowed by a hopeless love | Hallowed by a name | Swallowed by a golden dove | Gallowed on a flame.

Nothing wrong with anything | All is wrong with me | A lie meaning everything | Sin infinity.

Thought that slyly kills itself | Sigh-zero of death | Panther times panther of stealth | A murder in breath.

A fire that none can see | A singular flame | That is the fire for me | One, my only game.

Pressed under oceans of glass | Specimen of love | No more sun nor air nor grass | No return above.

You will not hear, will not say | For that life is hard | Silence upon silence flays | This corpus of words.

Angel too wants everything | In a special way | With a clear new voice that rings | The mirror of day.

Today is the last last day | Tomorrow first first | Earlier was not OK | And now is the worst.

My blood in a golden bowl | A great mystery |
Drinking it would make us whole | But you're not
thirsty.

This is how to kill the mind | This what to do |
This is all we'll ever find | This is me or you.

Antenna-top transmitting | Signals of our shout |
One needle knitting | Thread of the way out.

Time to leave, time to depart | So I think and say
| But all's so full of your art | That I stay and stay.

The stars that fell from your hand | From which I
fire took | May they never ever land | Or be named
in book.

You go your way I go mine | Under floors of sea |
To meet at the end of time | Neither you nor me.

Were I to leap from the edge | What else would I
find | But another lower ledge | A more narrow
mind?

Horror is eternity | Inside the screamer | What is this world-dream to me | Without a dreamer?

Where all vision becomes flat | The ocular square | Where everyone's blind to that | As if being were there.

When at last this love breaks me | And desire is dead | Your word will roar like the sea | From my severed head.

You take yourself for a spin | Try to feel alive | While the ocean lies within | Drowning in a sigh.

I write and weep, quote and sigh | Trapped in a bubble | Made of body, breath, and mind | Deep under rubble.

Sun and moon, night and day long | Sea and earth and sky | All singing a song | You are born to die.

There are no words to express | The desperation | This continual distress | And rare elation.

Is this what you really are | Your actual state? | Or something's that gone so far | It can't know it's fate?

Mirror opens like a tree | While the flower dies | Branching bodies into sea | Deeper than our eyes.

Word abandoned to a glance | That's the fate of breath | To swallow lines of a lance | Piercing life to death.

Incense of a thousand thoughts | Golden coral sighs | A trillion treasures unsought | Dropping from my eyes.

Not-today today as you please | The time never is | For unlocking golden keys | Treasures hers and his.

A tightrope walks my balance | Path to who knows here | Footsteps above such silence | Have nothing to fear.

To see light falling slower | Than a single thought | To know Beauty as knower | Of all things and naught.

I see you where I am not | Also where I am | Like the sea in a fish caught | Light of wolf and lamb.

Split into one like all else | There's nothing special | About a lost heart that melts | The fires of hell.

When your tongue loses its eye | And the eye its tongue | Where your ear whispers a sigh | And the heart is lung.

Smarter than all I can say | Is what speaks to you | Listen to it point the way | Beyond me or you.

Name nothing with your last breath | Now put it to rest | Abolish all facts of death | In a final test.

Thinking far beyond this life | Living beyond thought | Soul unsheathes itself—a knife | Piercing through this knot.

One pulls one via zero | Sum more than itself | A pure birth of my hero | From this dark world's filth.

A murder took place last night | Without crime or law | Killed and killer died by fright | Seeing what none saw.

Strangest sense that nothing is | Desert of the real | Then scent of that wine of bliss | Which all things does fill.

To wipe the soul-window clean | Full empty of mind | Drive through the world's triple screen | And leave it behind.

Life gives itself to living | And living to it | Until the gift stops giving | And dead is the split.

Swimming always at this speed | Between drops of breath | Generates strength beyond need | Living dying death.

To leave all and follow none | Outside space's sea | To stay right here and meet one | Inside the edge of me.

An horizon of fire | Reflecting the gaze | Of one whose real desire | Is to fly the maze.

I burn, burn, and burn again | It's all one huge pyre | Of flames searching through the rain | For the source of fire.

The alternate universe | Where this is published | Is probably worse | Than this one—I wish.

The universal pivot | Holding consciousness | To this wayward mess | O God whatever is it?

The more obvious it seems | That I should not talk | The further these verbal dreams | Take me for a walk.

Weep over oneself weeping | Losing all to do | Leap over oneself leaping | Rising like the dew.

Eaten by an alien | Because non-hostile | Trying communication | So predictable.

Emergency abstraction | Deaf pose of cool thought | Tripping out with no traction | On its own dark plot.

Turn out to have been nothing | Zero all along |
Exhume it all from something | Not singer or
song.

Losing the war with language | Lost the war with
thought | Near empty the gauge | Knot tying the
not.

Truth not what I tell myself | So cut out this
tongue | On the continental shelf | Near my heart
and lung.

The more common sense I make | The more mad
this sphere | Is anyone not a fake? | Yes—and
we're not here.

Usual suspect, own worst | Enemy, you choose |
What is the correct, the first | Term for we who
lose.

Words mean nothing, not even | What they really
mean | Just something to believe in | Between
death and dream.

The way you are interested | In what you're into |
Proves life to be dead | At least spilt in two.

Stop yourself before it stops | Die before the bomb | Explode all before it drops | Sing before a song.

Erased from life by two eyes | Haunting my own ghost | Among all stars in the skies | Of these who may boast?

It doesn't fit life or death | It cannot be worn | A scent not leaving my breath | From midnight to morn.

To speak of this is not true | Or false if you know | A lying sign for the few | With nowhere to go.

It is one thing to not use | Treasure one has still | Another to always lose | What one never will.

On the summit beyond time | That is where to meet | Everywhere life climbs | Worlds beneath our feet.

Time fills gas, stone, and metals | Dilating anew | Eternal virgin petals | Seeded with God's dew.

Who sees eyes I do not know | This double feature | Universal studio | Of all creatures.

Bolt my head to your threshold | Drill through my third eye | Everywhere vision is cold | Save this home of sky.

Body wax, breath wick, mind flame | I am the fire | Of the candle of your name | Lighting my tongue's lyre.

I'm so happy that you'll know | For eternity | The one in whom all things grow | Love's reality.

Charlatans of tomorrow | Avoid like the plague | Here is the end of sorrow | Paradise today.

To have wasted so much time | Until this today | Tasted all nothing of mine | As drives you away.

He sinks into the seaweed | Reads it as your hair | These lines are both net and reed | Ditties of despair.

From golden threads of absence | Poor love weaves its noose | Gift for suicidal prince | Leash of magic goose.

There is a hole in your heart | As deep as the sea | Set your pupil in the dark | Look the whole is me!

Since this life can't ever die | And was never born | I'll waste myself in love's sigh | From morning to morn.

No way to do, feel, or think | The all that I know | Less spectral than rose's pink | Black-whiter than snow.

Who knows if that was your glance | If this is your hair | When one's this trapped, so entranced | Does it matter where?

Clearly I know not love | Else I'd not be here | Speaking from below above | Words no one can hear.

I pretend you are present | Apostrophizing | As truth one who came and went | Philosophizing.

Tongue without an intellect | Heart without a soul | Will with no cause or effect | Neither part nor whole.

Spinning space like a spiral | Whirling round a heart | Laid out like something viral | On a one-wheeled cart.

What it is like not to be | Learn now from the soul | Growing all things like a tree | Toward the goalless goal.

Stars at my feet, head in earth | What am I to do | But surrender to this birth | Upside down for you?

Write the Divine Comedy | Beatrice don't care | Knows too well her Ptolemy | That Earth's way down here.

Delete all things ever said | Let them fly away | All contents of every head | To see what I say.

Dialogue with nobody | Heard by one and one | A spiral pile of debris | Burning the wet sun.

All's too much for those who are | So let's now away | To that lovely black star | Brighter than the day.

Let no one hear what I want | None believe desire | Need needs drink its very font | The spring of all fire.

The sonic booms battering | My waking dream door | Is your silence shattering | All I've known before.

All that matters is what melts | Iron mind to gold | A fire real in blood felt | By hearts young and old.

Mercenary of zero | Mannequin of art | Haunted being the whole hero | Hunted by your part.

She conquers all with a flower | Kiss cuts off my head | Draining origin of power | No one now is dead.

Everything already done | Nowhere not to go | All fights now forever won | Killed the final blow.

Forehead to forehead a jewel | Passes in the air |
Rippling our reflecting pool | With wrinkles of
care.

Burning column of fire | Locked inside a stone |
The fountain of your desire | Imprisoned in bone.

No one wins the game of love | All die as it starts
| Horizons flame with the dove | Burning impaled
hearts.

Dizzy in the spin of spheres | Drunk on no one's
wine | Lost among too many heres | Kite without
a line.

Only one thing on my mind | One word on my lip
| A spear so sharp and so fine | None can see the
tip.

What's everywhere the sleeping | Can in no way
see | A dark dream blocks their peeping | Like the
surface the sea.

Originality ancient | Splendid as a sun | Never
came and went | Older than none.

An angel swam from heaven | Walked on earth to stay | In me saw her reflection | And flew far away.

Nothing by the dream was seen | Neither you nor I | One was simply on the screen | And then the film dies.

After all it is still now | Before time itself | Before all I simply bow | After being a self.

The way all talk shows me that | Each has yet to see | For no one's word arrives past | The blind lie of we.

Becoming prayer without word | A logical breath | Love-servant without a lord | Past longing for death.

With a wind I fall off world | The transit of skies | Scanning eddies whirled | By your falling sighs.

Retract every thought, word, deed | Each experience | Now are you at last relieved | That nothing makes sense?

Waiting where there is no place | Not to move nor stand | Suspension here has no space | And the ground no land.

A question bigger than all | The answer appears | A secret whisper too small | For anyone's ears.

Head and feet and hands and heart | Climbing up the sky | Feeling from finish to start | Mountain is a lie.

In the well of tears was born | A fish with one eye | Hooked now by the rose's thorn | It swims through the sky.

Place all things in a glass dish | Weigh them in your eye | See that anything you wish | Isn't worth a sigh.

Swallowing still the lozenge | Sweet that swallows me | Gulping prayers of a stonehenge | Sunk beneath the sea.

I walk a name wondering | To whom it belongs | It wanders my squandering | Of love, thought, and song.

Speak no more of busyness | Your exciting plans | Heart wants truth not giddiness | Friendship real not fans.

It always knows more than you | It stays by your side | It is devil or friend true | If love kills your pride.

Fall to this floor in an X | Burn vision with tears | Open body beyond sex | Drop all hopes and fears.

Recall scents that never were | Unborn lights of eyes | Soar memories that never blur | Watch them split the skies.

The water drop refused me | When dying of thirst | Is now become a vast sea | Drowning best and worst.

Wherein lies the first demon | Intellect or will? | At last now knows the human | Whose zero one kills.

Escape your way without me | Crucify the God | On new planets one will see | Who is in the pod.

Working, writing, and weeping | Are my futile three | Ways to wait without sleeping | To keep watch for thee.

Everything knows I am wrong | That itself is truth | A lie lacking where I long | For pity or ruth.

To stand here wholly alone | On a furthest star | To twist space-time in one's bones | And know where you are.

Signals sent nowhere by none | Translated to this | Words unmeant except for one | Whose silence is bliss.

You are the one punishment | For all things in time | Embrace this paradise-sent | Gnostic paradigm.

I will find you in my dust | Touch you in the sky | Conceal you in my lust | See you in my eye.

My blood sings with secret fire | Except it's not mine | More like no one's desire | To be you sans time.

At least no one to speak to | That is a real joy |
Flowering the wall sky blue | Neither girl nor boy.

Reply is impossible | Where love is concerned |
Like fire inevitable | To one too soon burned.

Now that world is drowned in sorrow | Time for
something new | A today without tomorrow | Just
for me and you.

A species of ancient imp | An arch-trickster true |
Inverse voice of our throat-lump | Vanishing like
dew.

On second thought forget me | Cross me off the
list | With love for making one see | That I don't
exist.

Take not a lifetime to learn | That this is not life |
Blow the fire until it burns | Through you like a
knife.

About time now to catch up | To eternity | To
drink from the timeless cup | And from nought be
free.

A dream died eastward again | Apocalypse city |
The flood's sky also sank N_____ | What not
a pity.

End is nigh. Evacuate | Your life. The deluge | Is
now here. Do not be late. | There is no refuge.

Fun to attempt to converse | With oblivion |
Losing telegrams in verse | To a black hole sun.

I live here where no one lives | Metropolis void |
Where the undead raise kids | And art is a toy.

Rhyme everything with silence | A new word
appears | Pure war without violence | Opening
deaf ears.

The folly of desire | Written on this face | Will
melt fast in the fire | Consuming our race.

Sharpest shard of total light | Wrapped into a ball
| Playing hard at being night | To have space to
fall.

Dreams prove that experience | Is not what you think | More like a mirror of sense | Which you try to drink.

They pretend to have arrived | They say this is it | All while being flayed alive | In burning black pits.

A body is a shadow | of a shadow of | A shadow of something now | Something about love.

You are the truth none may prove | And I am the same | Endless movement none may move | Our own little game.

This no one's one reason to live | Is to be a way | For paradise to give | Its bird itself today.

To live right in the center | Of the piercing spear | The whole your heart will enter | When silence it hears.

Our dream is beyond this world | That much we do know | Who cares where the flag's unfurled | Whose names on it sewn!

I am breathing and breathing | Someone's secret name | I am burning and burning | No one all the same.

If you hear words you are wrong | Good or bad, this or that | This is an actual song | A true living fact.

Never again to say things | Because the God hears | No need to pluck naked strings | Of infinite ears.

Wish truth would just sit you down | And say all I feel | Then you'd burn to be its gown | And forget I'm real.

No time to write the epic | This will have to do | A no one, your weird relic | Burning all for you.

This life ends, syllables end | Breath expires, sighs die | One thing is forever friend | This is not a lie.

That this love is killing all | Is a highest joy | An eternal shout and call | Of one small dead boy.

If my tongue now leaves this world | Shoots beyond the blue | It's word will only unfurl | What you ever knew.

A ladder lowers itself | From the tip of this | Upside drowning what is felt | To harmonic scales of bliss.

Now speak to me of nothing | Dial topic zero | Float the sense of everything | Away with an O!

Journey is ready to depart | The last words are read | Brimming gold the burning heart | Transmuting all lead.

Happier than I dare know | Pure light of despair | Writhing in the endless glow | Of one's golden hair.

Gold upon gold upon gold | Is the pupil true | Sold upon sold upon sold | My black heart for who.

Our text is a weeping dance | A joy twisting black | Spinning void into a trance | Flight on wings of lack.

No stating the state of things | The fix one is in |
No point to a song that stings | Love whose prayer
is sin.

There's nothing this singular | Perfectly itself |
This species-less and this pure | Not in heaven,
earth, or hell.

My love loves nothing of you | Way too much for
sure | Bolt of gold out the blue | Poisoned with its
cure.

Future of abandonment | Destiny most blind |
Surrender to an accident | Of infinite kind.

In intolerable fire | No way to be me | But me
screams I must expire | So both drown at sea.

Were the mountain infinite | That would be the
best | For then one might leap from it | Never
come to rest.

An endless spiral coiling | Around no one's heart
| The monstrous ocean boiling | Corpse and soul
apart.

Because today one leaves me | I must leave me too
| Half alive under the sea | Dreaming of him and
. . .

Never the heart's inflation | Will once ever stop |
A universe-dilation | Only NOW goes pop.

I stopped before the setting sun | Saw what none
should see | A man still looking for someone | As
if he were me.

The space of this my body | Neither here nor there
| Dimensional oddity | A curl of your hair.

Becoming one desire | Living in one lack | Sparks
in the world a fire | That time's bell will crack.

Whatever the inference | Whatever the view |
There's no greater difference | Than twixt thyself
& you.

Spontaneously one sees | And sometimes is veiled
| Yet for this vision to please | Tis best to have
failed.

Crystal fount of endless tears | Oceans of desire |
River flowing beyond fear | From eternal fire.

Time to take experience | So seriously | That no
one gives not two cents | What happens to me.

Stretch everything to a skin | On which all is writ
| Peer upon who lives within | And whose eye is
it.

I see the day, see the hour | Now see this moment
| And not once the whole power | Round which
time is bent.

Place me where all horizons | Will now cease to
be | Far beyond time's denizens | And eternity.

Broke the box where all is kept | Nothing was
inside | Only a weird thing that wept | Without
mouth or eyes.

Fires of a trillion eyes | Embering the blue | Pupil
black beyond all skies | Searching all for you.

Spend me like gold in a world | With nothing to buy | Lose me like a stray hair curled | Near the edge of your eye.

I am one who carved your eye | Wove your skeleton | Now I will learn you to die | So we may be one.

Only thing I think about | Is a strange new sphere | Far beyond belief or doubt | Where all things are here.

No way for being to be | And that's how it is | That's why the waves of the sea | End up just like this.

I left a long time ago | And still never left | Say thee yes or say thee no | It's all a giant theft.

Everything steals everything | Hides it in itself | Spiraling each thief and ring | Riches without wealth.

Left is there and right is there | Back forth and up down | Yet only indifference cares | If you smile or frown.

Union of separation | Omnipresent spear | Narcissus speculation | Desert ocean tear.

An angel wearing your face | Leaped out of the block | Her wings gold with crimson laced | Where this head was chopped.

One day soon I'll learn to leave | The labor you set | Upon my sweaty brow's sieve | When we never met.

Now life nearly never was | I feel strange sadness | For no reason than because | My greatest gladness.

Count it not a miracle | Nor natural thing | When the God empirical | Requests that you sing.

To think that one ever thought | That one ever sighed | To feel that one ever sought | That one ever died.

A dream danced me off the cliff | Past the pupil's doom | Now I fly on fires of if | Burning the same room.

All that one might ever say | All there is to feel | Flowing now like blood away | From a tongue unreal.

Dying death that cannot be | Ever living now | Pure impossibility | Without why or how.

To fail this miserably | At doing nothing | To lose inevitably | What there's no escaping.

Void bubbled into a point | Point into a sphere | Now all is all out of joint | In the center of here.

Do you want to feel happy | Be glad all the time? | Then why not ditch that crappy | Body-spirit-mind?

Indifferent to all and it | Good luck making friends | One too loving for your wit | Too light for your lens.

A thing that hangs all night long | On a thread of name | Woven from smoke of a tongue | Echoing a flame.

I wear a name round my throat | That no one can
see | A leash-name to choke a goat | Til no one is
me.

An unfading light and scent | Of eternal air |
Never came and never went | True gold without
care.

You have touched body and sensed | Spirit and
mind thought | Now see that all, thick or dense |
Are shadows, naught.

From atop a false summit | You shout out your
name | Or the sound of me is it | Falling from the
same?

Shoot a bullet through the dream | And it dreams
the hole | Strike the bell and let it ring | For whom
it now tolls.

Time only happens in time | Where nothing
happens | Save the space it takes to rhyme |
Counting nows and whens.

All shall be well and all shall | Be well tomorrow |
As today all's swell | Swallowed in wells of sorrow.

Not by thought, feeling, or act | Is this treasure
found | Only by its own sheer fact | Buried in
one's ground.

Now folly and unfolly | Have fallen to fight |
Everywhere all is folly | Without day or night.

Threw myself from way up high | And flew back
to me | Drowned myself in the black sky | And
became the sea.

The love that is killing me | And is killing you |
And killing all that we see | That's the love that's
true.

Because lighting is so fast | It lasts forever |
Splitting in a single blast | What can't be severed.

Like a purest golden pin | In corner of I | That's
how thou art held within | Me until eye die.

Observe how all people live | Observe how they
die | See the one that none can kid | To whom they
all lie.

Press the button that says here | And feel the ground shake | Now press the one that says there | To hear sky awake.

Have felt your seed in my blood | Seen it in my breath | If only its flower will bud | Someday before death.

No more words, never again | Not one syllable | Nouns never come to an end | Verbs are too painful.

That seems to be the whole point | To be without care | Starting with whether or not | Any point is there.

Praying for I know not what | Hanging on a thread | Scanning the world for a dot | Neither live nor dead.

Extinguish the Milky Way | Blot out the whole eye | Should I fail to live a day | Forgetting to die.

No more words, never again | Not one syllable | Nouns do not come to an end | Verbs are too painful.

And what do you hope to win | What game do you play | Down here among the ruins | Of what does not stay?

Forget goal, kill origin | Drown the whole damn show | Leap the path into a spin | With nowhere to go.

Destroyed by what never was | Dunked in an abyss | Of total causeless because | Without even this.

To die deep in a basement | Of the heart's high head | And live as the replacement | Who knows that it's dead.

Zero pupil of each point | Black sun everywhere | All-present ocular joint | Neither here nor there.

Lamenting in a green glade | Knight became a pest | So all the animals prayed | That he end his quest.

This tiny cell my ocean | Bigger than the world | Round it origin and end | Like a spiral curled.

Open the tall blue bottle | Where the tears are kept | Sprinkle them in the dark vale | Where they were first wept.

Summit arrow sigh rebounds | Striking the sky's bell | Music falls without a sound | Making all things well.

Whole world alone with itself | Solitude of none | Sphere between heaven and hell | Burning one in one.

Suddenly see the weirdest | Nothing ever seen | Like some vast blank palimpsest | That will always been.

This whole life never happens | Did nor ever will | It sleeps through itself like sand | Blowing nowhere still.

Now to enter paradise | One is first bent straight | Like a needle without eyes | Through the narrow gate.

Pierced in the midnight moonbeam | Of a throat-lump world | Pupil swallowed the whole dream | And coughed up a pearl.

Your name is a sword, a star | An endless flower | A word calling near and far | Your name is a power.

'All my friends fell out with me' | Even I and you | 'Because I kept your company' | For no one is true.

See what you are up against | An eternal fix | Immaterial so dense | That nothing can nix.

Practice nowhere, theorize | Nothing beyond this | That is how to see your eyes | And to drink their bliss.

Dervish spin the spiral drill | Boring through my heart | Sit so impossibly still | That all falls apart.

You are the ground I lie on | Face down in the dust | Dreaming of our love's heaven | Beyond spheres of lust.

Everything is on fire | Each form is a flame | A shape of endless desire | A sound of your name.

To erase the book of life | In a single glance | Is the effect of your eyes | Beyond circumstance.

Now that nothing ever happens | All over again | And abysses that never were | Have always been crossed ...

Where is where and when is this when? | And who breathes your air | Atop an all-sinking summit | Never won or lost?

Hand that reaches through all dreams | Grabs one by the throat | Wrings out your life through its seams | Hangs me like a coat.

Absolute bewilderment | Anonymous sigh | Acosmic imprisonment | Abjection of I.

Love secret beyond belief | Telegram of none | Unfathomable relief | Circumference of one.

Happy to be born, happy | To forever die | Happy not to be happy | Happy not to lie.

Saw the see and heard the hear | Therely was there | Nothing next to being near | Your sweet breath of air.

Body of you in the air | Walking through my being | The warm chill never not there | Melting all seeming.

Far be it from me to be | Among any first | Better to sink in this sea | Best to be the worst.

I have seen the universe | Your presence empties | Heard the voice blasting all earths | And drowning all seas.

Treasure born for burying | In the dark cold ground | A gold one is carrying | Never to be found.

Goodbye all and hello one | Now a time die | Living like the whitest sun | In the blackest sky.

Over life before began | Origin no end |
Infinitesimal span | Swerve without a bend.

Answer's absence is answer | Silence on the wall |
Writing like a small dancer | The name of my call.

Unkillable polar bear | Kills my morning dream |
Day haunted by its dead stare | An unscreaming
scream.

The world is not of this world | Nor any other |
Spiral around nothing curled | Abortion mother.

To renounce all for nothing | No reason at all |
Suicide no one breathing | The scream of a fall.

Sang gold pillars into being | Nemesis plummets
| Miniaturized all seeing | Around three summits.

Desire forbids desire | On pain of desire | To be
other than desire | For its desire.

You who cut my spinal cord | You who mapped my sighs | You who erase my toward | You who never lies.

Your beauty is pure zero | Nothing but the all | Still bleeding from an arrow | Shot through my eyeball.

I will be here forever | Thinking still of you | A head that can't be severed | Eternal and true.

Only the exhausted ones | Ever taste this love | Their desiccated bones | Drawing dew above.

Death by individuation | Perfect upside down | Headless translation | Empyrean crown.

Impossible to explain | This crystalline sea | Surrounding islets of pain | Bliss aquamarine.

Suddenly lungs are a swan | Flying the abyss | Whitening the darkest dawn | Of all that I miss.

When the one looks straight through you | Then one clearly sees | That the one thing really true | Is not I or we.

It swallows itself in crowds | Social chaos swirls | Enveloping in its shrouds | Little boys and girls.

Bouncing between white box and black | Father and mother | We overfeed the forge of lack | Its fire smother.

Strange feeling that strangeness feels | Placeless abduction | A cure-all that nothing heals | Harmless concussion.

Straighter than straightness | Truer than truth | Ancient greatness | Eternal youth.

Spiral evisceration | Of the blinded I | Oceanic dilation | Of the weeping sky.

Time is water | Space is sea | Whirling ever | Spirally.

Tear upon tear | The drop of time flows | Year upon year | Eternity grows.

Alone at home with no one | Nor alive nor dead | A heart-shaped declining sun | Dawning severed head.

A bond that breaks all bindings | One golden thread true | Found far beyond all findings | Outside me and you.

An arrow shot beyond the sphere | Every atom thrills | A sigh set free to save one's life | Soon returns and kills.

There is no way out and you are it | No path to the goal | One lost chance to finish or quit | Single empty whole.

The constant turmoil of my heart | Is your tress's curl | No curve the one has, no art | Save the other's swirl.

To speak somehow without speaking | Of the weary self | To pour a heart without leaking | Self to selfless self.

I have aged seven thousand years | In two or three days | I have found the ocean in tears | And lost all my ways.

Plant yourself at the root of all | And weep your eyes out | Perhaps fruit unseen since the fall | From the top will sprout.

The one who wishes he could say | But can't so he does | Is one for someone on this way | Towards the last because.

The sight of that pupil-eclipse | Is the brightest sun | A fire where all fire slips | Melting into one.

Beloved hallucination | Self-deception real | Paradise imagination | Ever open seal.

The lion consuming my heart | Is becoming I | His crimson mane now wholly part | Of the dawning sky.

Beyond the legends of being | Outside dark and light | Into the black of all seeing | Eye inside the night.

Abandonment times abandonment | Sanctuary of none | Totally endless bewilderment | Transinfinitely fun.

Float all day in the tomb of bliss | And all nighttime too | There's nothing in the world to miss | Neither me nor you.

Being crushed by black hole gravity | Of heart-fire in a box | Fashioned in a glance of purity | With one key and zero locks.

A stream of tears through the center | Of my forehead | A window for one to enter | When I am dead.

What violence I have done | To myself in this mad love | What destruction no one won | Losing below and above.

Monster to oneself is I | Evil incarnate | The longest slow way to die | Or be born too late.

I am the essence of all disease | The cause of every ill | Forever impossible to please | My name is your own will.

In the swirl of bewilderment | In a well of pain | Somewhere above the firmament | And inside the rain.

I breathe fire thinking your name | My gaze forever gone | Trapped inside the one living flame | Of the most distant dawn.

A blind insight scratched out by | Fingernails of fate | A nice long life without why | Gone before too late.

Nowhere to turn, nor to hide | Nothing to be done | Only die a thousand sighs | Drowning into one.

Thing that never goes away | Until all things do | This madness, this mask, this play | Twisting me and you.

No one sees me where I live | Except a love I'm not | Nothing receives what I give | Apart from a lost thought.

The sap flowing in this tree | Seeps to be cut down | All the drops filling the sea | Crying out to drown.

Love looks into a mirror | You enter his eyes |
Whoso perceives this treasure | Neither lives nor
dies.

The only news is word of my beloved / The only
sword, the one cutting off my head.

If you know what I cannot say | I do I do I ... |
Then maybe there will be a way | To die to die to
...

Swim the heart one cannot speak | Forget about
air | Except the lost spheres that leak | From your
mouth and hair.

I'm flying home in a tomb | Lined with your
glances | Resurrecting in a room | Born from all
chances.

They say I am looking well | It seems you are too
| Perhaps heaven's way through hell | Leaves no
trace or clue.

Wash all my blood away with tears | And my tears
with blood | Evaporate these days and years | Into
one pure flood.

Hidden idol of my heart | Ever present friend | Tearing the temples apart | Unveiling the end.

Life weeps eternal at your tomb | Dying of beauty | Seeing everywhere is no room | For this endless sea.

I was there and now I'm not | Once upon a time | Zero over which all fought | Cut the only line.

Nothing but life to live for | Only death to die | Everything a single door | Without rhyme or why.

Not enough to live and die | Not enough to weep | Not enough the earth and sky | To wake and to sleep.

I walk among nothing | In beauty never fed | Down pathways of splendor | Without mouth or head.

Stars of my eyes touch your tongue | Syllables of light | Soul strings with soul itself strung | Saliva of night.

Only the forever close | Can be this away | Far far far nearer than most | Night when it is day.

Fact that I am writing this | Futility true | Hyper-ordinary tryst | Without me and you.

Believe no one who complains | Deafen the sad din | Trust only silence that rains | One tear from within.

My body is your body | Every breath your breath | Of someone not she not he | Ever living death.

Blinded by the lance of life | Breath its trickling blood | Thinking only the flame's light | Body soul kabob.

Pluck my ocean-seeping eyes | Wash them in the dust | Drown all but one of these sighs | Burn the flames of lust.

Fire in my hands and feet | Fire in my eyes | Fire in my bones and meat | Fire of the skies.

Suck the poison from my soul | With a little smile
| Then swallow the candy whole | As I die a while.

The fact is that I am now dead | No longer here
nor there | A severed heart swallowed my head |
And sighed up all the air.

Run forth to where the heart flies | Sail on
feathered feet | Swim far beyond the mind's eyes
| To where we will meet.

At the center of the eyes | There your dark one
dwells | Gazing fire beyond the sky | Burning
heaven's hells.

Things simply do not happen | How you think
they do | Whim is the only fashion | Eternally
true.

All light adorns your darkness | Galaxies your
womb | All color sings your blackness | Each
flower your tomb.

Maybe better not to speak | Hold golden silence |
Perhaps wiser not to leak | Raining lost guidance.

So this what it is like | To live without life | Riding no rider no bike | An edge with no knife.

If only one had not sighed | When there was a chance | A way finally to die | And not on this lance.

Never mind my thoughts which are in flesh embedded | Recall the heart where your arrow is beheaded.

The dream is twisted like twine | Round the pole of love | A spiral ribbon divine | Below and above.

Was not there when I was born | As I'm not here now | And will not be when I'm torn | An eye from this brow.

Dawn of sparrows on our street | Singing golden sky | Flying where we always meet | No one's paradise.

As you are beauty and I truth | Ever good is our kiss | Too bad these mouths are tongue and tooth | Born *inter faeces et* ...

To give up all experience | Embrace the crystal death | To think and feel only silence | With each and every breath.

Whatever this is or not | Above/below the sun | Nothing escapes being caught | In a truth that is one.

It is not, not at all normal | That anyone ever lives | Just the property most formal | Of what none receives or gives.

You are a sorrow and a joy | Nothing that real is | A yesterday of tomorrow | Like nobody's biz.

If I loved I'd not desire | If not desire not love | O the paradox of fire | Burning o'er itself above.

Species of insanity | Face of the unreal | Perfect selfless vanity | Illusion's own seal.

To be more than a being | Along for the ride | To give all without seeming | Ever to have died.

Things make sense to you because | You don't understand | That all rules, norms, codes, and laws | Are way out of hand.

We is begging tomorrow | From the futureless | We is buying free sorrow | With our happiness.

And instantly now you know | All one never did | See everything high and low | That from eyes is hid.

Only one who is betrayed | You by you by you | One flaw of all that is made | Who by who by who?

Perish thought or perish me | Abolish the coin | Drown hazard in the heart's sea | One to the one join.

Poison lozenge of pure love | Sucking all hearts dry | Fanging worlds on worlds above | Through the whyless why.

Swallow self until it pops | Poison one's own well | With sweet saliva that drops | From the roof of hell.

Let sleep fall asleep to sleep | Waking itself wake | Let dreams over dreaming leap | Thought its poison take.

There is nothing to see here | Even less to show | Only an absence too near | Someplace never home.

If I were me and you were you | All things as they are not | Reality would be less true | Than the truth where we're caught.

One thing for the pain we are in | Is to dance dance and dance | To tarantellize the poison | Is our only chance.

The ocean finds no room to drown | Fault is per se mine | Amigaras all the way down | Abyss hell divine.

More lines re: inevitable | Impossibility | More rhymes re: inconceivable | Incurability.

You know who your true love is | Even know his name | Why then do you fail the quiz | And live on in shame?

Now that this life's finally over | And nothing's left to say | I'd like to invite you over | On the next final day.

In the beginning—nothing | Just as there is now | And yet that is everything | Without why or how.

Here the one to whom you turn | Inside the turning | Here the one for whom you burn | Inside the burning.

Pay now the price for not dying | While there still was a chance | Gulp down the pain of not lying | Before love's holy lance.

In the tornado's midst | I tear worlds with your name | Blowing storms with a kiss | That only feeds the flame.

To die so many times | That one forgets how | To walk so many lines | That there's only now.

I remember all the steps | The dark in the hall | All the heights of all the depths | But not, not the fall.

I place me where I am not | Swim a glacial tide | Look down on life's so-called lot | And laugh where I died.

You know the one who will be there | When your throat is cut | You love him who does not care | And never does not.

Maybe want nothing at all | Slow up to max speed | Yes no suffering no fall | Just infinite need.

Sit with earth until it blinks | Alone with alone | Float on air until it sinks | Spirit into bone.

No one ever thought a thought | No one wrote a word | No one learned the lesson taught | Or said what was heard.

Never too late not to have been | To return above | Never too late to lose and win | In other words to love.

Kill me while I'm still alive | Not when I am dead | Make a bullet of your sigh | Shoot me in the head.

And there will you be again | Casting down your eyes | Forgetting the only end | Hiding the surprise.

In the end I am so glad | Not to be or do | Not to be happy or sad | But that there is you.

Cosmos is hypocrite | Betrayer of form | It acts like it is it | Where there is no norm.

Go ahead and try to say | What it's all about | I'll meet you beyond the way | Where there is no doubt.

As if everything is lost | And no turning back | Infinite the final cost | Charged against pure lack.

Relax this first time in life | Drown upward on death | Pursue all war beyond strife | Breathe the ocean's breath.

Impale the spear of desire | Drown in virgin tears | Liquify at root of fire | Make afraid all fears.

Say real words that truth wants to | See all thoughts at once | Drink open the morning dew | Embrace love the dunce.

Say real words that truth wants to | See all thoughts at once | Drink open the morning dew | Embrace love the dunce.

Ever gaze at all your books | And just fill with tears | At the thought of all those looks | Drifting through the spheres?

Why weep when you can be wept | Flowing ever new | Why keep when you can be kept | By what's truly true?

Tell me never the reasons | Of the sky, sky, sky | All the smiling horizons | How they lie, lie, lie.

Flying flat through my third eye | Burning all clouds of fears | I touch you with antennae | Of golden spiral tears.

And if you did understand | Still, what is there to do? | Below is nowhere to land | And you are falling too.

Seems I was going somewhere | Or so I once
thought | Now see there is no here here | And all
is as not.

Heart as a suicide bomb | From beyond the
spheres | Its fuse one universe long | Burning
days months years.

Beauty misdrew her image | By thinking of it |
Now her wings look like a cage | And her smile a
bit.

Unfold my heart from the sphere | And lay it out
flat | I'd like to see where is here | Without world
or map.

A wound I bleed swells with blood | Deepest
darkest well | The eternal rose its bud | Paradise
its hell.

That which always never there | Without knowing
knows | That which breathes all time like air |
Eternally grows.

Tell me not I am mistaken | To always think of you | That this rare dream must awaken | To see no one is true.

I see through doors of blindness | Fainting from your sigh | I grasp in death your kindness | Never knowing why.

Not even no one to talk to | And everything to say | More than everywhere to walk to | And not a single way.

Freeze the lost flow of my mind | Petrify my heart | Wire them in a name that binds | Blow them both apart.

Missing life and missing death | Whatever in between | Murder victim of each breath | Neither seer nor seen.

Golden blood of living fire | Perfume of the stars | Undawning formless desire | Horizon of scars.

Forget you to forget all | All to forget you | Leaving falsehoods to the false | Their truths for the true.

One who knows my desire | Who will set all free |
The same who is the fire | That is burning me.

To wake up inside the walls | In between all things
| Where the road to nowhere calls | And the last
star sings.

You are His and He is thine | Beyond possession
| Truth eternal for all time | Beyond confession.

I hear your name in every line | Writing like the
wind | An air unwinding the pole of time |
Without and within.

A life living by surrender | Of all that is alive | A
sigh flying oceans under | The highest summit
dive.

Like a fish out of water | Or star out of sky | An
unlimited slaughter | With no one to die.

Alien shock of beauty | Color from beyond | New
spark of ancient duty | Our all-breaking bond.

A million nuclear missiles | Of pure missingness
| Times as many silent whistles | Of pure
kissingness.

A crystal gaze murdering | All objects of view | A
sigh ever whispering | Below deepest blue.

Infinite unsent letters | All addressed to you | A
slave's self-fashioned fetters | Windows beyond
view.

I am standing now forever | Holding time and
space taut | Love-joined to a cut that severs | The
real from what is not.

The demon is chained to a stone | Tempting you
to come near | Whose fault if you enter its zone |
And believe in its fear?

How on earth to stay right here | Counting on
nothing | To live live live beyond fear | Inside this
crushing.

Were I to remain silent | For million million years
| Could my tongue say the secret | Once
whispered by your ears?

Undersea crystal cavern | Located through stars |
This life become its prison | A breath now its bars.

This crossroads of life and death | Trembling
element | This hyper-perilous breath | A near-
fatal scent.

Lost in a maze of sorrow | All but infinite |
Yesterday and tomorrow | Simple hypocrite.

I claw through all earth for you | Burying myself |
Threading a golden hair through | Paradise and
hell.

A thousand days of weeping | Finally cracked my
skull | Now to follow the seeping | And swim out
through the hole.

Fever locked inside a tomb | For a thousand years
| Constant motion without room | Fire of freezing
tears.

Nicola is not someone | Who may speak his heart
| A candle snuffed by the sun | A line blown apart.

Your name is the brain tumor | Of a dying heart |
At least that is the rumor | Spreading through
these parts.

A million seconds, minutes, days | On empty
vacation | Lost in the vast, self-centered maze | Of
imagination.

Funambulate the sword-edge | Abyss of despair |
Stroll to the paradise ledge | On a strand of hair.

Eternal mistake of a lifetime | A perpetual sin |
This constantly falling endless climb | Of the X
one is in.

Where the only thing you want | Is what you will
never accept | A kiss from the very font | Of every
tear ever wept.

Drowning in a sea of wounds that heal | Losing
taste for air | Swallowing the matter all forms feel
| Eating hunger rare.

Obliterating every breath | With thoughts of no
one | Liquidating all life and death | The earth,
moon, and sun.

Pay no attention at all | To fear or to want | Let
every ghost play until | It is they you haunt.

Misspell me until your ear | Whispers to my heart
| A thing your fair eyes most fear | The point of
their dart.

Break never this golden thread | Spiral pure of
hair | Growing both ways without head | Lifeline
to nowhere.

Melt in absolute wellness | In God's mouth like
ghee | Bore through bottomless hellness |
Swallowing the sea.

Breath is so drowned in your name | All air is
marine | Space the surface of a sea | Time a sunk
machine.

Only way to live without you | Is live without
myself | Only way to think about you | Is think on
something else.

To dive to the ocean floor | Glimpse the only pearl
| And swim on to the earth's core | Forgetting the
world.

The illusion is massive | Deeper than all dreams |
A vast actively passive | Web woven of seams.

Timeless cube of pure vision | Crystal mirror eye
| Place spark of one heart within | See universe
fly.

You are not my confessor | Yet to you I speak |
Carving pupils in a door | For the friend to peek.

Sunk so far in the ocean | Swimming between us
| Breathlessly certain that none | Have ever been
us.

Now that life's over and death | Is not left to die |
I can stop to take a breath | My first and last sigh.

An indefinable style | Never loud nor dim |
Spontaneous sundial | Cosmic clockwork whim.

Ripple of a single drop | Pulsing through the
sphere | The slow universal pop | Turning there
to here.

Only one game everywhere | No one playing it |
One word all syllables share | No one saying it.

Not wounded, a walking wound | Cut in time and
space | Perforation of ground's ground | Void-
blossoming face.

Silent evacuation | Of pleasure times pain |
Farewell to goodbye station | Love alone remains.

Unwitnessable face-to-face | Pure asymmetry |
Most tragic rift in time and space | Emerald
beauty.

Look around and try to find | The world we all see
| Anywhere but in the mind | Of not you nor me.

Go ahead and make a fuss | Tell all how you feel |
Words will never convince us | What they say is
real.

Clarity of one's whole life | Passion transparent |
Restless peace and warless strife | Breath on
mirror spent.

At risk of saying something | I'll say I love you |
That way all our ears will ring | With a lie that's
true.

The end is a beginning | Outside the center |
Losing the way to winning | Exit to enter.

Nobody on Earth is cool | Especially you | Except
that one nameless fool | Who alone is true.

Love kissed life into the dead | Waited near the
door | Then fast without a word fled | When I
wanted more.

To suffer at last in silence | All thought and all
feeling | To no longer flee the violence | You from
you are stealing.

Sick in body, heart, and mind | Dying from a
dream | Of being one who might find | Truth in a
moonbeam.

To lose what you never ever had | Before it is way
too late | To succeed once at not going mad |
Before they open the gate.

Monstrosity to impose | On another desire | As if someone else's hose | Might satisfy fire.

To float this far with no clue | Where one is going | All thanks to a missing crew | That can't stop rowing.

Before you cut off your own head | Beg God to remove it | Then live on forevermore dead | So that He may prove it.

To commit the only mistake | Again and again | Until . . . nothing. One day the snake | Dies in the garden.

Boil thyself down to black slime | Seal it in a jar | Now wait as deep space and time | Make of you a star.

To open this dark cell's door | First locate the key | Feeling for it on the floor | Conscious misery.

Unwind this throat lump of gold | To a million spools | Weave of it a robe eight-fold | For the King of Fools.

Love chokes life and death to death | Sucks their blood and sighs | Breathing into both new breath | One that never dies.

Once I saw my friends laughing | As if they had lives | It was like photographing | Bees dead in their hives.

If you know this restlessness | Perhaps we should talk | Drift in silent deathlessness | Or go for a walk.

Leap over the opposites | Fly through zero's hoop | Spin as the spiral that twists | Time's Möbius loop.

Look never for what you want | Avoid desire | Kiss now the one kiss, be blunt! | Toss fire on the fire.

See how I am cut you say | Therefore I am real | Loosening a tongue which flays | Worlds that never heal.

Discuss your plans with no one | Above all yourself | Walk fast and straight on the one | Road to perfect health.

You know not even the half of it | The sighs, the tears, the swoons | The appalling dark side laugh of its | Melodramatic moons.

Want that kills all other wants | Making all kings slaves | Ghost haunting all other haunts | From beyond all graves.

One whose form is in your heart | His heart in your face | One whose style is in your art | His art in your trace.

The God appearing between | The sun and the moon | Is the very same one seen | That day in your room.

That you are is way way way . . . more | Than what you'll ever be | Yet there fits through the latter's door | The first's infinity.

The green water of a soul | The blood of one's life | The breath of existence whole | Your faithfullest wife.

Beware feigned simplicity | The flat-modest stance | Cloaking a technicity | That can't really dance.

Put on one's own murder case | Assigned to this birth | Called to report back to base | Somewhere beyond earth.

With your hands extract my tongue | And with it my heart | Making sure the wings, my lungs | Do not fall apart.

Buried under the horizon | Every here nowhere | Pierced the pupil of all eyes on | An infinitesimal hair.

The only dust worth the name | Is dust of your door | Only fire worth the flame | That which does restore.

All resemble what they love | Though looks may deceive | Each below follows above | As sharer or thief.

To always fail everything | Again and again | To constantly lose the ring | Of not having been.

If you are now reading this | It means the quest failed | To rescue from your abyss | The self you have jailed.

Shall I live not to see it | You will still see Him | And touch and taste and be it | Source of every whim.

Spinning fast into a fire | Of high branching hymns | Swimming far above the pyre | Of our burning limbs.

The universe is a seed | Planted in the ground | Of a planet without need | Never to be found.

Live the strangest experiment | Never knowing why | Experiential testament | Of no one to die.

I have seen earth, moon, and sun | Inner, outer space | Many shadows of the One | Never once your face.

Now to be this mistaken | Is not possible | Unless I'm to awaken | From circles of hell.

I am still glad that you are | Even if you're not |
Happy birthday to a star | Before time forgot.

Here now stand on brink of being | Never mind
the mind's word | Fly an arrow through all
seeming | Shouting the oneness heard.

Golden noose around one's neck | Which alone
life gives | Liver for a bird to pick | Where one
never lives.

Step away from life and death | Spin into a ball |
Spiral to the peak of breath | Long before the fall.

Dawn-woken in a crevasse | Body-mind broken |
Thank love for this true impasse | Real silence
spoken.

The stars falling from my eyes | The fire, the tears
| Are higher than all the skies | Longer than all
years.

Stream up to the water's source | See what a
thought thinks | Circle back to the first force |
Taste what the wine drinks.

There is just one thing to find | To see, taste, and hear | Not body, spirit, or mind | And it is right here.

I feel the end of all time | Hold it in my hand | Like an invisible slime | Of sea, sky, and land.

It's still today when you die | Razoring the night | It's still this way when that sky | Has been put to flight.

Appalling melodrama | Dark bureaucracy | Lovely shock-and-awe trauma | Scorched heart policy.

One in the heart is present | Single possession | Never received, never sent | Perfect obsession.

The clarity of your eyes | Untellable dream | Extraordinary skies | Invisible seam.

Clearly known what real love needs | And still you refuse | Like some sick poet that leads | To hell his own muse.

I've received the gift of sorrow | Pulled out all my
hair | And still there is this tomorrow | With you
standing there.

Nessuno knows who I am | Specialmente me |
Hang questa carne like ham | In Parma, Italy.

Now that folks have had their say | Let them keep
quiet | At least for one single day | Without that
riot.

That for which you all day sell | Mind, body, and
breath | Is a little taste of hell | The eternal death.

See how it is all a trap | One enormous trick | A
science-fictional map | Infinitely thick.

Nothing to have but the One | Forever and now |
Burning to dust every sun | Without why or how.

Your veil is all desire | Your pupils the night |
Blinding eyes in the fire | Of a sword of light.

Bound still by the same blinding bind | Bereft of any rift | Caught too cracklessly high to climb | I fall not, nor freeze—drift.

Lifetime shoots through the ceiling | When is found your word | Thought flying beyond feeling | Arrow never heard.

That sweetness unless tasted | Never understood | On which all else is wasted | Is our only food.

All-nourishing love-lozenge | Golden lump in the throat | During longer than Stonehenge | Edible asymptote.

Face the face all the way down | To the first cavern | Where a smile kills the last frown | And the sky is tavern.

He walks earth to set us free | Ghost beyond measure | Fire of one melting we | Into the treasure.

Long all day shout in silence | Cross the mountainside | Smiling down on the violence | And the place one died.

Born to death inside a chain | Linking earth and sky | All life climbs by joy and pain | To the whyless why.

Art of living without limbs | In a jungle wild | Losing head and heart to whims | Burning moth-man-child.

Longest no longer ever | Alone with the none | Where is the sword to sever | The two into one?

Like strolling back from straying | Past no-return point | Like rolling forth from slaying | The soul-body joint.

Only truth could be this wrong | Only light this dark | So beyond music this song | So not fire this spark.

Far less a rudderless ship | Than shipless rudder | Not so much a slipping grip | As sinking shudder.

The candle explained itself | While the table wept | But there was joy on the shelf | For the secret kept.

Thus murdered by this marvel | Of a bleeding sky
| Thus flayed a human larval | Into butterfly.

In the white tomb of this love | In the lightning
flash | Nothing seen below above | Universe of
ash.

Fall down earth of gravity | Climb up fire of flight
| Convex all concavity | Solarize all night.

Before you were I made you | In the madness free
| Now pass the fire to fade you | Between I and
me.

The word is a soul-hunter | Tracking this life
down | Glad to be slain ere winter | Split navel to
crown.

Shortcut to infinity | Or infinite maze | Elected
affinity | Of you and your days.

A shield of gold is lifting | Between east and west
| A stream joining by sifting | The worst from the
best.

Even if they could secure | Every want and need |
Nothing would the fear assure | On which their
hearts feed.

Carry me in your pocket | Tuck me in your breath
| A tiny weightless locket | Souvenir of death.

To never ever get it | Dying before birth | To meet
what never met it | In this life on earth.

Feed the fire that all burn | Drown the dry of wet
| Fail the lesson that none learn | Win the lose of
bet.

I am sitting where no one | Left no one for here |
The lost city we all won | When fear lost to fear.

As if I were another | And you not yourself |
Worlds without world forever | Pure subjunctive
hell.

Now there is no life nor death | Neither no nor nor
| Only you for whom all breath | Once breathed
itself for.

Say no more the things of time | But weeds and flowers | All the lost plantings that mime | Eternal powers.

I do not want to exist | Whether false or true | On this only I insist | Just to be with you.

Everything is over now | That ever once was | How is that possible, how? | Only just because.

Spilling life into spiral | Funnels of despair | Over nothing gone viral | Into everywhere.

Lock me inside a mountain | Bound with crystal names | Of every sun | To burst into flames.

To die from wanting to know | Simply where one is | To finally overthrow | Space of all that is.

All my thoughts are of someone | Who does not exist | One whom I have lost and won | The top of my list.

At first I wanted to live | Secondly to die | And now is the time to give | Up both without why.

Run run run run run away | Faster than you can | One all love is here to stay | Not woman nor man.

Tis a total mystery | Sorry but it's true | No such thing as history | Of me or of you.

To be without anything | Emptier than space | Amounts to everything | Before this one's face.

They lie about everything | About nothing too | Above all the love that sings | Between I and you.

Desperation to die for | An all-tying twist | No more oceans to cry for | Dereliction tryst.

Be utterly mistaken | About good and bad | Stay blind to the truth taken | From this life you had.

And then just as suddenly | Everything stops | So that hyper-cunningly | The fall itself drops.

So today one just might live | Indeed, for once, here | Nothing to gain or forgive | In the mirror clear.

Forget it all from best to worst | Close yourself in a pod | Spiral through the universe | And belong to the God.

Entangled with the body | Confused by a mind | Wrapt in coils of energy | Seen through this soul blind.

Scrying through the photographs | Til appears their twin | Walking like someone who laughs | The air death is in.

Moving firm in the knowledge | Tasted in each breath | Both near and far from the ledge | That oneself is death.

Enough felt and enough thought | Enough done and said | Enough won and enough lost | Enough live or dead.

Acute golden arrowhead | Sharpest memory | Anagogy-encrusted | Subjectivity.

Dancing yes beneath it all | Groundless discotheque | Leaping fly into pit fall | Broke abyssful neck.

All that we will ever lose | Always never was | Now stand knowing well to choose | This without because.

Suffering the consequence | Of first suffering | The endless tip of the lance | Of this golden ring.

I am the head of all your limbs | You the soul of my head | Thus by a light that never dims | We never will be dead.

There is no economy | No culture, no state | Only the metonymy | Of what's on your plate.

The one who has seen beauty | Is no longer I | For that is its true duty | To pierce through your lie.

The constant thought of my heart | Non-stop perfume drip | Poisoning every step's start | Biting each word's lip.

You are as an ancient sea | Like the very air | Too far away not to be | Found everywhere.

This slowly one is broken | To want nothing more | Than to hear nothing spoken | From the furthest shore.

Thought I was full of desire | But it was hot air | The fume of nothing on fire | For something not there.

Hype-o-crisy vanishes | In this sphere of light | Whose thrilling eye banishes | The pale black of night.

Were there ever any way | It is now gone now | Just like one forgot to say | When we would ask how.

The spirit of those lost hours | Permeate my poor heart | Like new scents of ancient flowers | Born not of nature's art.

Desire of mountains, mountains | Of desire | No matter more light or more dense | Transhuman fire.

If the heart is torn in two | Then where might one
be | Save swirling inside the blue | Deep within
the sea?

In this crystal chest of mine | A gold compass cup
| Dug from the shaft of earth's spine | Always
pointing up.

Perhaps today I will not | Do what I have done |
Namely roll from thought to thought | Never
touching one.

How long will you shy away | From what you now
know? | How long may a plant delay | That which
makes it grow?

So this is what it's not like | To ever exist | To walk
the line of a strike | On no one's non-list.

A plain simple pine hyperbox | Knotted with
desire | Sappy tomb of one who still walks |
Perfect for the fire.

I rest here where there are none | Wondering
what to do | Blaming this earth, moon, and sun |
Everything on you.

Thinking is the worst idea | Shortest cut to pain |
Unless one knows how to be a | Dust mote in the
rain.

Scratch everything ever said | Scratch out my own
eyes | Scratch the horizon that once bled | Colors
of your sighs.

Life of spirit nailed to wood | All blood, sweat, and
tears | Unseen in a world whose food | Is
nourished by fears.

Very glad not to announce | Anything at all | To
have no reason to flounce | Other than this
scrawl.

Hope to have never met you | But that is insane |
Seeing that all's one not two | And I am to blame.

No one shall make eye contact | With someone
and live | Fire is the only fact | Zeroness will give.

Totally dead forever | Alive and kicking | At the
gates of a never | My throne is licking.

That from which tornadoes run | That which the void fears | That which sleeps inside the sun | That which each swerve nears.

Tis more akin to madness | Than to sanity | Tis far nearer to sadness | Than to vanity.

Infinity of errors | The wayward abyss | Sublimity of terrors | All ending in this.

Then one day the ghosts wake up | And decide to be | Smiling like a golden cup | They were you and me.

Dream of the dream of the dream | Waking beyond you | Seem of the seem of the seem | Opening the true.

Life and death are simply that | As all other things | Facts so infinitely flat | They fly without wings.

By unfathomable ways | I draw you to me | Sewing all hours and days | Through eternity.

To fail this abysmally | Beyond conception | Without possibility | Of less deception.

Stab at the sky with the tip | Of a slit heart-knife | Blab the last sigh with a lip | Of split apart life.

All things always pass away | Inside turning skies | Save the light that ever stays | Unseen in your eyes.

I am myself no other | Eternally me | Everything's twin brother | And sister so free.

I would say it's too too bad | But then then again | Who am I I to be sad | Anywhere or when?

At the bottom of some river | A statue turned to stone | Its all-petrifying liver | Brighter than whitest bone.

Thus without realizing it | One threw life away | Leaving little in the pit | Where you went astray.

Sorrowing over nothing | He finally went blind |
An auto-vampire sucking | One out of one's mind.

Whole penetrated a point | Neither one survived
| Just the X of one new joint | Of motion deprived.

Trace all back to the summit | From where we
once fell | Step footholds of the plummet | All the
way through hell.

Float in the tomb forever | Past matter life
thought | Above the passing weather | Of what is
and not.

The fact is only love loves | Not anything else |
One spirit of many doves | Music of the bells.

Seems the number one obstacle | Facing
humanity | Is a massive lack of people | Not
embarrassed to be.

What seemed for sure to be a fault | And sheer
waste of power | Was in fact a grand somersault |
To save one small flower.

An idol tripped in place | Shattered where it stood | Now to the sun turns its face | To the sea its blood.

And suddenly the river froze | Flowing into a void | Petrified by your laugh which rose | From dust of hope destroyed.

So it is oneself who betrays | Oneself in every case | Presuming fixed a star that strays | Set the mask of a face.

I am the face who appears | Within all real art | Shining through the veiling spheres | Of a sincere heart.

Point dies and becomes a sphere | Strangling all my sighs | With expanding shrinking fear | Of your pupilless eyes.

Seems the river's passing by | But you're swept away | Under the bridge that none try | To a sunless day.

So from now on say nothing | Silence understands | Swallow this plus everything | Strangle one's own hands.

Everything I could say | All that I might do | Is nothing next to that day | When no one met you.

Cotardian taxi ride | Leaving biosphere | Via spirals no one sighed | Still remaining here.

Summoned by a special doom | To this fateless fate | Invited through the worst room | To a waitless wait.

I was never there nor here | On this all insist | Whispering in everyone's ear | You do not exist.

Lost in a dream of the real | Sunk in purest fog | Buried under the king's seal | In a crystal bog.

Wrong to think, to feel, to act | To do anything | Wrong not to leave all intact | Touch the virgin spring.

I will stay with the sparrows | Loving in the dust | Where heart touches its arrows | Between blood and rust.

All this while on the sea floor | Breathing through two eyes | Until my lungs cut a door | Opening the skies.

Drowning seas of endless doom | Sighing seas of skies | Floating in the truest tomb | Upon unseen eyes.

Nothing to say to no one | Yet still babbling on | Thinking the stupendous sun | That all have forgone.

What they say at your funeral | None of it will be true | You are proof indisputable | That none ever knew you.

To still be alive is birthday | In this alien sea | Where nowhere is to swim or stay | Only dive to death of we.

Nothing the matter with truth | You are the sick one | Biting with a rotten tooth | And a bitter tongue.

Heart out of my body swam | Taking all with it | Elsewhere in the sea of AM | Under suns unlit.

Life ended aeons ago | Before it began | On a lost star you will know | At the dawn of man.

There is nothing for you here | In case you missed it | This becomes terribly clear | Once you have kissed it.

The universe is a veil | Wove of nothing fine | Which to see one's eyes must fail | Of I, me, and mine.

I murders all that you love | For the hell of it | Sinking below and above | Into one flat pit.

No longer know what to think | About anything | Draw the scorpionest blank | Stung by blackest sting.

Nothing to look forward to | Nothing to regret |
Soon now it will be anew | The first time we met.

I have tried a million ways | Will try millions more
| To lose the scent of those days | Flying on the
floor.

Since love rules the universe | We are in trouble |
Until one's absolute worst | Explodes this bubble.

On your knees frail humanoid | Admit your defeat
| Say hi to the smiling void | And kiss its pure feet.

Separation's fact sinks in | Life dribbles away |
Down a slow drain that drinks in | What will
never stay.

You are real and I am real | Never having been |
Imagine how it will feel | When all now is then.

The tongue of a hungry heart | Flaming through
my chest | Is starting to lick apart | New lips in
my breast.

Only truth knows what is true | That's enough for me | The rest of I, they, and you | Can drown in the sea.

Slowly slowly slowly now | Climbing free of all | Lowly lowly lowly how? | Fall by fall by fall.

Darkening under the strain of | Impossible desire | Then purified in a rain of | Paradisical fire.

I sing to the single fire | Piercing through all eyes | The music true of the liar | Inside each disguise.

Hear what my veins are saying | Not this twisting tongue | The name our blood is praying | Thinking of someone.

How bear waiting any longer | For what is forever? | How to dare becoming stronger | Than what none can sever?

Recall one's in a theatre | Sitting upon throne | Whether being him or her | With none or alone.

Looking for a breath of air | The kind someone sighed | On that today we were there | And I near you died.

Nowhere anything happening | Still all are missing out | Like some weird senseless flattening | Of what it's all about.

Seemingly infinite time | That is what it takes | To walk home out of the slime | And kill all the snakes.

These words worse than your silence | Syllables of hate | Nailing home love's violence | On the door of fate.

Saddest thing to do violence | To violence of love | Violating its silence | With science of love.

Although it kill me and it has | I will remain headless | At the true feet of that topaz | Unalive and deadless.

I stake my heart on your heart | I on spike of eye | I kill my art with your art | Life with death of die.

People have taken over | Where the people are |
Love is snatched by the lover | Buried in a star.

Who else are you looking for | In light of this sun?
| What else think you is in store | Other than the
one?

Every moment is a door | Leading who knows
where | Ain't that more than enough more | For
any who'll dare?

If you are indeed so right | Then why are you
mad? | If you are so full of light | Then why are
you sad?

One thing all I ever want | Yet not one can see |
Anyone who might it grant | Not you, God, nor
me.

I float in a pupil tomb | Buried in your eyes |
Somewhere there's not even room | For one of my
sighs.

Endless quest for nothingness | Ultimate leap fall
| Twisted inverse willingness | Of the all in all.

I am done with you and me | Over the pronouns |
Dying in one without we | Until drowning
drowns.

I am with the ones who died | Trying to love you
| Not all the losers who tried | Wondering what to
do.

This world is pure friendlessness | That my true
friend knows | Someone sighing endlessness |
Past horizon's flows.

Turn every sea into blood | All air into sighs | The
whole earth into a flood | Of tears for your eyes.

Before you follow that flute | Until I obey |
Authority absolute | What words can one say?

Stay me always where you are | Chained here like
a goat | Til I feel the furthest star | Slicing through
my throat.

Lost all the ways except one | Erased every track
| Sole option the never done | Turn no turning
back.

They pride themselves on opinions | Brag about their luck | Ask for money, seek minions | And use the word f____.

To live and die in a dream | Never seeing why | The ice cream tastes like ice cream | The cave looks like sky.

Crucified upon hypercube | Strangled by a sigh | Drawn and quartered on the Danube | Are three ways to die.

So mistaken in all things | Let down by all/none | To whom is it heart yet sings | The dead legs still run?

Nothing better than what is | Worse than what is not | Optimus cheats on the quiz | Pessimus gets caught.

Remaining within all things | | By staying without | Dead certain about nothing | Beyond any doubt.

When answer a question poses | Be prepared to sigh | When song a nightingale roses | Get ready to die.

For sure the pain is endless | At least you are not | While the whole world is friendless | To end is its lot.

Mistake I'm making is me | Would that I never | Walked so far across this sea | Into the ever.

Unfortunately you are | And I somehow am | Zero cut horizon scar | Lineless diagram.

Now I see of what you're made | And I built the same | Just of what will ever fade | Body without name.

Sew me now into the fold | Of your garment blue | Within golden threads that hold | Souls tied to the true.

My body is a small tree | Like yours made of wood | Floating in the darkest sea | Of infinite blood.

Slowly the final sadness | Pervades every part | Purging the first, pure madness | From our whole heart.

Smart is to see stupidity | Above all one's own |
Savoring that sweet quiddity | In silence alone.

One only sees when one will | No moment before
| Not sooner than something still | Opens the
eye's door.

Torturous asymmetry | Cutting all in whole |
Askewness of you and me | Amputating soul.

To only speak one zero | Over and over | Until the
breath's last hero | Kills its first lover.

After the war in heaven | And the falls of man |
And God, there comes round again | One
remaining plan.

In order to find this place | One must cancel time
| Faster than a fold in space | Slower than
thought's slime.

Pearl in the well of my soul | Thrown in by the one
| Whose first look forever stole | All light from the
sun.

Love's labor is to suffer | To drown in the rain |
To swallow every buffer | Between self and pain.

Lives spent in spirals of dust | Lost in labyrinthine
| Games of anger, greed, and lust | Of I, me, and
mine.

The pleasure of being is pain | And pain is not
pleasure | And yet I AM is not insane | To think
itself treasure.

Love loves to encounter love | Trap itself in its net
| To show below and above | That no one ever
met.

To live within an open wound | Inside outside
near | Dwelling like the tiniest sound | In the
vastest ear.

Since there is nowhere to turn | And nothing to
do | I will just sit here and burn | Not forgetting
you.

If you cannot see and tell | Truth's real truth
within | Yourself, where is that but hell | Some
blind pit of sin?

Know if I wait forever | My love will appear | Feel if I myself sever | You will be most near.

Takes this long to realize | Cause you still refuse | To zeroly synthesize | All one's points of views.

Standing still with all and none | Dying to know naught | Thinking of the only one | Out of nothing wrought.

Wondering about this flesh | How it gathers here | Molding around the mind's mesh | In patterns so clear.

God fill your body with light | Bathe it in pure bliss | For what else is this long night | Made for all who miss?

Never mind remembering | Never mind forget | Recollect dismembering | Recall this null set.

Being overwhelmed feeling | Is a big fat liar | Yelling help from the ceiling | While it is the fire.

Grind grinding to dust faster | This all seems too slow | The mill vaster and vaster | And no wind to blow.

Perceptible and the not dance | Swirling dust perfect | Touching near that core of this trance | Where all ships are wrecked.

This ocean is drowning all who | Like you or like me | Don't have nothing better to do | Than be I or we.

Marry the abyss within | To the void outside | Making love out of your skin | Like a spiral bride.

Transvertical ecstasy | Overhanging bliss | Drowning in the alpine sea | Of all things not this.

Since everything has conspired | To place life in the dark | We'll drink the wine of the tired | And sing dawn with the lark.

Is it not enough to be | In this universe? | Why on earth must you and me | Work to make it worse?

Living is hypocrisy | Except for the dead | And the life that drowns the sea | Swallows every head.

Life stirred, took a few soft breaths | And went back to sleep | Never knowing they were deaths | Too many to reap.

Beginning and end in one | Rolling like a ball | Single sphere of moon and sun | Flying spiral fall.

No beginning and no end | Absolute spiral | Swerving that to which all tend | Infinite viral.

Gem embedded in my heart | Impossible sleep | Excavating by your art | Futures far too deep.

Skeletize my stormy mind | Transmute thought to bone | Crushed by whatever will grind | Knower into known.

To no longer fail to fail | This fall fast enough | To out-freeze the swiftest hail | Be crushed beyond dust.

Way of life is weeping fire | Shouting silent sighs | Whispering beyond desire | The flames of your eyes.

See the sea-green horizon | Deepest ever line | Of hearts from which drip this sun | And the planets nine.

Kinda thing you gotta be dead | For which there's no way | As in cutting off one's own head | In order to say.

If perchance you understood | I would not exist | Such is the law of the good | Crossing us off of our list.

A few souls scattered here there | Thinking of the one | Whose description includes hair | And deeds beyond done.

Thank God love lets me love you | The way love knows how | Otherwise what could one do | But never be now?

Line is a crack in the shell | Point is a pupil | Curve is a place none can tell | Sphere is the apple.

Hard to tell what's happening | If something at all | So massively unending | So wall-lessly wall.

Not this that it's everything | As if it were not | Something not stopping breathing | Decaying all rot.

The reality is that | This is where we are | Not on some earth round or flat | Orbiting a star.

Saga of everyone's dreams | Leading death to death | Transforming sighs into beams | Shining crystal breath.

Lose everything nothing to lose | Drown last bubble of mind | Swimming deep into yellow blues | Breathlessly flying blind.

This feeling, this thought, this thing | Inescaping me | That irremovable sting | Poisoning the sea.

Ocean tried to catch itself | And became a fish | Hopelessly hooked on the hell | Of that very wish.

The world thinks I am joking | Proving I am not |
Its laughter is my choking | Its blooming my rot.

Horizon is the sea floor | Vertical flatness | Spun
into an alpine shore | Of steepest thatness.

Spiral back into the shell | Tie all in a knot | This
paradise point of hell | Time that space forgot.

All seeming lost of all gold | Gone the very thing |
This unconquerably old | Singlessly song sing.

Pulled from grave by dream of you | Desert by a
drop | Of love dripped in chalice true | Down from
mountaintop.

This nothing whatsoever | This purest of flame |
All zero moving lever | A silence of name.

A whisper more real than all | Sweet breeze of
your void | For one sip slips the whole ball | Its
axis destroyed.

One who tasted this treasure | Now lost voice and tongue | Hanging days without measure | Where no song is sung.

Wax bodies, wax breaths, wax thoughts | In the sun all day | All beings alive and not | Now melting away.

This only thing that remains | One eternal truth | After all pleasures and pains | Before age and youth.

Blank slate quarry hunting boar | Who once pierced your thigh | Knee-bar crux dihedral door | Of the bloody sky.

Tiniest drop of true gold | Hanging by a sigh | Soul-thread of the knight made bold | On a lance to die.

Thrill my throat-lump with a sword | Pierce it with your name | Cut this point opening toward | Source of every flame.

This is not the other world | That one is not this | One into the other curled | In a knot of bliss.

As if something to say | As if not all said | As if life for one day | As if not now dead.

Still holding to your doorstep | Wanting death to end | Not grasping this lack of help | Is itself the friend.

Circulating through your heart | The silence of the skies | Visible in every art | The thorns of your eyes.

Tornado took off its head | Throat-lump swallowed heart | Now the stump not live nor dead | Splits itself apart.

How come you can't live and die | Like you're supposed to? | Why must you weep, blab, and cry | Like the other fools?

Order space back to zero | Tell all time to still | I am sick of this shadow | My own stupid will.

Fact of you erases me | Atom at a time | Until never traces be | Perfect silence crime.

Must be what it is to be | Somehow to exist | A breath drowning in no sea | Bubble zero kissed.

To sit in the dark with life | For an hour or two | Without peace and without strife | Wondering what to do.

Without knowing beforehand | No scent, track, or star | Walking straight into no land | Neither near nor far.

Perpetual disorder | Nothing in its place | Cosmos-clue of the murder | Of having a face.

Were there any wiggle room | I might squirm to you | Trailing silent cracks of doom | Cross the sky so blue.

Never again talk to me | Nor I once more to you | There are no words in this sea | No syllables this blue.

Once fallen off the cruise ship | Hard to get back on | Best to forget the whole trip | Dive into the dawn.

Admit infinite defeat | See you are all wrong |
Amputate head, heart, hands, feet | And burst
into song.

And to think I thought this joy | Somehow
paradise | Not an infernal alloy | Of fire and ice.

Losing the thread of all things | Dissolving this
breath | Unravelling the dark strings | Of birth
and of death.

Turns out I was a tantrum | No more than a cry |
Some moaning blabbing phantom | Above all a
sigh.

I want there to be something | And yet there is not
| Not even this one nothing | None ever forgot.

Must stay on river bottom | Not float up through
floors | Wash away as stone fallen | To where the
sea roars.

Cosmic balloon tragedy | Hardest all to bear |
That heart of one's gravity | Is only hot air.

All is burning with the fact | Of being this far | So sunk outside every act | So starlessly star.

Between silence and the blasts | A slight chance of bliss | Enjoy while it does not last | Inexistent kiss.

Twas love until you said I | And ruined itself | Swallowing the sigh of sighs | With these words of hell.

I not for me not for you | I no one one knew | I me not me through and through | I truelessly true.

Sound of corpse itself tying | To the river floor | Flow of life ever dying | Upon my heart's shore.

Amputate yourself: cut a ring | With the knife of the heart | Slice everything from everything | And save the better part.

Go carefully now, steady | Given all we've seen | Take your time to get ready | Never to have been.

Two scoops, of birth and of death | In one sugar cone | Served with a spiral of breath | And sprinkling of bone.

Someone/something to speak/hear | Were there I might say | Or better as in this sphere | Still in silence pray.

So the best thing I can do | Is no longer be | That is, forget me and you | And simply now see.

Swallow the heart of failure | Inhale ownmost worst | Drown today like a sailor | Let the bubble burst.

Infinite gratitude kiss- | ing infinite grace | Totally eternal miss- | ing no one's pure face.

Nothing to worry about | Stop boiling your brain | Silence cures all fears and doubts | The world is insane.

The saddest thing to occur | Without occurring | All things now a buzzing blur | No flower, no sting.

One must take all one's veins out | Replace one by one | After spiraling about | That order of sun.

Nightmare wants nightmare to end | Staring at the sky | Seeing not the stars are dead | That it wants to die.

Yes this wound was already there | When opened by your eyes | Yet with what arrow, through what air | Did they pierce from inside?

Split compass needle stuttering | In black spiral chasm | Broken moon moth fluttering | Unrecorded spasm.

Went to where the people are | Saw a lot of things | Like the most near labeled far | Puppets pulling strings.

Indeed it is mad to speak | Yes I am a fool | But it's the vessel that leaks | Which makes water cool.

God forbid that one should speak | Express anything | There is no word, sigh, or squeak | Worth the silent sting.

Since there is no way to say | Silence alone is sane | Do me a favor and pray | I never speak again.

Sit with self in empty room | Until no one speaks | Shows the way out of the tomb | And slaps both your cheeks.

The only one to talk to | Has cut out my tongue | Lost every place to walk to | Set alight my lung.

I think I know what happened | Died and then forgot | That that was indeed the end | And all this is not.

Body itself is the door | Not what walks through it | To find out what it is for | First you must chew it.

In order to stand without | What you are not in | Simply peel back every doubt | To its origin.

Another thing scarier still | Lurking in your pain | Is that you never were nor will | Be yourself again.

If all things were not other | Than they are not now | Then I would never bother | Or even know how.

Put nothing into action | With each single step | Attend to no attraction | Over yourself skip.

No one owes you anything | Nothing one can give | Save the life of everything | That alone will live.

No matter how you slice it | Or how hard you try | Or with what name you splice it | Only the dead die.

I used to know how to live | And now I do not | How to receive and to give | Or so I once thought.

Spill me like a cup of wine | Uncork my vessel | Empty this of I me mine | Or send me to hell.

Forget everything forget | There's nothing to see | Cancel everyone we met | There's no one to be.

After being what it's not | Oneself learns to die |
By passing back through its knot | The needle of
I.

How many times I've been here | Wondering
what to do | Being a being in fear | Of just loving
you.

I place the world to my lip | Take a little taste |
And with only one small sip | It's all gone to
waste.

Burn everything I said | Except you know what |
The body of words has bled | From one tiny cut.

Suffer silence in silence | Persist in love's love |
Pass through pain and violence | Here below
above.

Breath of life and life of breath | Woven round a
name | Become cord binding to death | The heart
still aflame.

Problem is I'm still thinking | Playing with my
head | Not with a whole heart drinking | The wine
for all bled.

Soon as there's something to say | No one to say it | Soon as there's nothing to pray | Someone to pray it.

Where imagination meets | Real reality | And the highest alpine feats | Fall into the sea.

Inside marble of your tomb | The burning white stone | Within fire of your womb | Post-eternal home.

In golden wings enwrap you | In powers divine | With highest love entrap you | Free of every line.

To pour oneself out into | Happy happiness | By swallowing all doubt through | Empty emptiness.

God is love and love must love | But for that to be | One sees below and above | You and also me.

Drift in seas unknown to men | Sail upon the thought | That every where and all when | Are nothing if not ...

The angel arrives faster | Than any can see | For
no one knows its master | Not you and not me.

To walk away from all else | Going anywhere |
Winding down winding itself | To a single hair.

Of nothing to be dying | Just another case |
Without eyes or mouth crying | Just another face.

Until everything happens | Nothing ever will |
Save this mysterious sense | That is with me still.

Vision is hurricane | The heart a vast sea | Waves
are pleasure and pain | The ship you or me.

Bullet in the head of all | Divine pill of void |
Secret love and dread of all | Death by life
destroyed.

Stay with what stays, flee what flees | Press your
heart's flower | In the book of truth and ease |
Into real power.

There is nothing to do here | Point is to use it |
There is no me or you here | Life is to lose it.

Pupil as the only one | Who will never see |
Darkness where what's done is done | For
eternity.

After the lance was removed | And the heart bled
out | Nothing remained to be proved | Nor room
for a doubt.

It will last a little while | And then it will die | Or
will itself through the trial | Never knowing why.

Dear friends and dear enemies | We are all the
same | Seeking only self to please | Spoiling the
game.

As if heart's not born broken | Every throat
formed cut | As if all's not mere token | Handheld
hazelnut.

There is all to discover | Nothing has been found
| Not one has raised the cover | At all from the
ground.

An error in the first place | Mistake in the third |
Ever second in the race | No one of the herd.

As it's between I and me | And there's no one here
| Seems this singularity | Needs to disappear.

Tell your troubles to no one | Above all who tells
| Specialize in having fun | Not in all your hells.

It inhales my exhaling | And exhales my in | Fails
to fail in my failing | And loses my win.

More not wanting not to want | Than a real
wanting | Less haunting than a haunting | By the
very haunt.

No wonder the friend left you | No wonder I cried
| No wonder we all fell through | No wonder they
lied.

Once believed there is someone | Now I am not so
sure | Either way it is all one | Universe without
cure.

Spirit of America | Spoke to me through dream |
In plain esoterica | Of life's passing stream.

I am the one who left where | The rest carried on
| A species who lost all care | For the always gone.

You are proof that none exist | Argument divine |
Against all that would persist | In the field of time.

In this body I am not | In that one I am | Like
some net in a fish caught | Or shell in a clam.

I saw the place where my life | Died by its own
birth | I walked the wound where your knife |
Drew blood from the earth.

Whole mad spiral of desire | Never ever where |
Burns the real, actual fire | Right here over there.

If only I had left me | Out of the whole mess | But
no I wanted to be | More than zero's less.

Time to go and no one leaves | They all hang around | Like a field of grass that grieves | For its very ground.

Strangest of strange places this | No one not grotesque | So on-target-ly amiss | Naturally possessed.

Say goodbye why you still can't | Spill over the rim | Of your non-stop stupid rant | And embrace the whim.

At least there is still something | One thing that exists | All that's left of this nothing | You crossed off the list.

Lovely high in heaven's blue | Scaling candid climes | Last thing you need me to do | Is count all our crimes.

Never wanted to be one | Preferred to be split | Now that life is said and done | That was simply it.

The hardest thing in the world | Until you do it | Bitterest pill ever pearled | Unless you chew it.

Used to think I was alive | Now I know I'm not |
Bee unborn inside the hive | Life that life forgot.

Sitting alone with this gem | In a secret cave |
Hanging from the highest hem | That alone will
save.

Unless head under your foot | Cannot think a
thought | Until top is one with root | I not all I got.

I climb upward with my eyes | Weep with all my
pores | Fall through the ground of all skies |
Laugh through all the doors.

I missed the chance long ago | And just now again
| Maybe not by tomorrow | I'll miss it again.

That which saved my life killed it | You know what
I mean | Once tagged you are always it | Ever
dying green.

Heart is a universe wide | Thus vaster than that
| A space beyond all spheres sighed | Eternal
format.

Now that I've always lost you | To who you are not | It's time likewise to see through | The me that me sought.

A flame made of hardest stuff | Or I am too soft | Dumbest iron black and rough | In fire's ice tossed.

Because there are no people | Especially you | Because the human pupil | Is faithlessly true.

Skin of starlight, voice of black | Universal hair | Drawing all forward and back | Into everywhere.

Invisible you appear | To all who would see | And more closely you are near | More we cease to be.

My love is the lord of all | And your beloved? | Mine if here I stand and fall | Now forever dead.

Heart hoarse from silent screaming | Raw and torn inside | Eyes blurred from endless dreaming | Of the life I died.

Reached out to remove the mask | Hand pulled off my head | Thought of a question to ask | Answer shot me dead.

The word that dropped from my tongue's tip | And burned right through my chest | May it pass the door of your lip | And die inside your breast.

Send yourself on an errand | Never to return | Fall into the fire and | Don't forget to burn.

This life is a special kind | Of inexistence | An irreplaceable find | Of perfect nonsense.

As long as I am not here | I might as well be | A way has nowhere to steer | No exile the sea.

I am you and you are me | That is simply true | Now we need the mystery | To show who is who.

Of course I am so stupid | As to want something | Only weight pulled by Cupid | Is one's own damn string.

Part of resist not evil | They don't understand |
Cheek of a slap uncivil | Stain cutting your hand.

I hate life and it hates me | We are all the rage |
Performing our enmity | For none on this stage.

I have nothing to give you | You nothing to me |
Except maybe one small true | Drop of sanity.

Think by cutting off your head | Breathe holes
through your heart | Live insofar you are dead |
Tear yourself apart.

Feels somehow that one is lost | Someone always
found | Treasure searching for its cost | Upon
empty ground.

Things weren't going well until | It just seems that
way | Now that your shadowy will | Is seen by the
day.

Pick yourself up by the heels | Drop it on the fire
| One thing no one ever feels | Is real, true desire.

Utter fiction of someone | Interested in you | In anything you have done | Or will ever do.

Only path to tomorrow | Stay in today's pit | Only way beyond sorrow | See that you are it.

The whole thing hit such a nerve | That all of life shook | One massive black spiral swerve | Of an endless hook.

God walks the museum still | Letting anyone | Freely murder him who will | And it's never done.

The one who knows my secret | True lover of love | Is someone no one once met | Far below above.

Since when is desire friend? | Since when will it help? | Shall the pearl-diver ascend | Entangled in kelp?

Never once acted wisely | Towards life as a whole | Moved constantly most shyly | Around the real goal.

My whole life is undersea | You spy just a breath | Few bubbling spheres left of me | Long after this death.

This is what it does not take | To make it through life | Inedible piece of cake | Uncut by a knife.

One million percent hopeless | Every step a fall | Or so I like this ropeless | Alpine climb to call.

I will stay here forever | Still thinking of you | Until the never sever | The false from the true.

Slime trail of crystal sorrow | Piercing no one's eyes | Leading to this tomorrow | Today paradise.

No more communication | All word is now dead | Chronic logos castration | Silence severed head.

Another great dead stab at it | One more dying boast | Parasitic blab at it | Desecrating host.

One day I will wake and see | That it's all a dream | Unwinding oneself to be | A thread of the seam.

Wrong turn taken everywhere | How else to be here | Twixt earth fire water air | Never in the clear?

Love is dead and so am I | Yet we keep flying | A bright burning in the sky | Of the undying.

Weep me off my feet until | These eyes touch the soul | Swoon all spheres to sleep so still | One awakes the whole.

I'm hanging in your silence | Strangled on your name | Swinging high in the violence | Of love's little game.

Last thing I should ever do | Think another thought | And yet it now happens through | Exactly when not.

Perfectly impossible | In all directions | Paradise descent to hell | Abyss erections.

Does not matter who I am | What the hell you do | No one knows to no one damn | Soul is one and true.

This is just one little life | No way all there is | So shut up and sheath that knife | A blade not yours—His.

I pass along before you | Passing along now | To find new homes for the who | Without knowing how.

In the hollow earth of heart | Near the dying night | In the nothing at the start | Near the missing light.

World of which we know nothing | Space wherein we fly | Hurled who knows where by something | Finding place to die.

A life still living once dead | Is my gift to you | A heart-sighing severed head | Impossibly true.

Cut loose the infinite list | Of all left to say | Or it might drown me adrift | On this wayless way.

Take me in your hands like clay | Knead it down to dust | Make nothing of me just play | As long as you must.

The end is faster than you | Speedier than time | Utmost arrow straightest true | Between eyes of thine.

Never leave home with yourself | Remain on the throne | Sipping from the summit shelf | Alone with alone.

No friendship in/with this world | Serpent swarm of lies | Or simply my true face curled | Into snake disguise.

Must now say goodbye to me | So goodbye to you | Happy somehow the one sea | Will will all we do.

If there were something to say| Anything to do | My command would have its way | With all except you.

There is a situation | Unlike ever seen | Its beauty is privation | And its eyes are green.

Herd blown hither and thither | Looking for a sign | Of the next whence or whither | Where to get in line.

And then it is all over | Now you suddenly | Are a new kind of lover | One that drowned at sea.

That which is surviving me | Neither live nor dead | Emptying into the sea | Stream-born severed head.

Hooked high on silence of will | Hanging by life's thread | Wondering how all is this still | Without being dead.

End everything all over | Again like before | Erase today forever | Until there's no more.

See the real reality | The one never seen | Live the true finality | The one never been.

For whose are you after all | At the end of day? | Into what arms do I fall | As I fall away?

The highest mountain of all | Was given to me | So began this lowest fall | Unfortunately.

Everything in everything | Save this little bit | A tiny shard of nothing | On which I now sit.

On wrong side of every thought | Searching here for you | Among shadows of dreams not | Even dimly true.

In the coffin of my dreams | Nailed within dark wood | Peeping through the leaking seams | At the sea so good.

There goes there being someone | There goes you and me | Welcome neighborhood of one | Goodbye zone of we.

Given that we cannot live | Surely cannot die | Guess now is the time to give | Up, not even try.

I pant after the music | Music chases me | Power-sigh of the lovesick | Breathing spicily.

Follow door into the clear | Leave the seen of crime | Dive this deepness of the near | Swim to here from time.

If had something to offer | Most likely one would | Too bad what's in this coffer | Is not all that good.

It was so wrong to assume | Something could be said | Yet this life leaves little room | For one to be dead.

In the secret of my sigh | In the gold of love | Burning to ashes the sky | And the sun above.

Constant mistake of thinking | There is someone here | Friend beside the fount drinking | And not empty air.

This awful abandonment | You do it to you | Every single moment | Thinking truth untrue.

Worry about the future | Today's delusion | Is the attempt to secure | A pure illusion.

No one has ever seen you | Especially me | And all that we have been through | Will never once be.

I am standing where you stand | On the selfsame shore | Offering you your own hand | Like I did before.

Watch me over waterfall | Flying past your eyes | Futuring the font of all | Amid newest skies.

Fleeing their own company | They go out at night | Finding faces so many | Full of the same fright.

That which once filled the silence | Is now the silence | That which erased the violence | Is now the violence.

Snow falling slower than time | With no snow at all | Nows murdering beyond crime | The fall of the fall.

My beloved is the God | Who got rid of God | She is neither young nor old | And our heart is Go( )d.

Grab one double gravity | Lust heavy light love | A convex concavity | Soul hand body glove.

Beauty lost and beauty found | Playing hide and seek | Spying its own face around | The curve of your cheek.

There is no ground low enough | Whereon I might lie | Nor a music slow enough | To measure my sigh.

Inside the lightning strike | That destroys my life | There is nothing at all like | Suffering or strife.

You wanted something for you | That is what you got | A clear sky, perfectly blue | Filled with all that's not.

I am nothing so are you | That is how it seems | Near the center of the true | Inside of my dreams.

You know who you are kidding | Saw it all along | Trying to do the bidding | Of something all wrong.

A history without time | The way it is now | A vast quiet cosmic chime | Without why or how.

Love is real and you are not | Time to face the fact | Erasing mind of all thought | Every word and act.

Sink yourself into a well | Fill it up with tears | Swim away beyond the hell | Of minutes, days, years.

Laugh so hard the universe | Vanishes in fright | Weep so deep the very worst | Remedies the plight.

Who killed who I cannot say | But the we is dead | Bleeding out where one heart lay | From two severed heads.

Sit me near the brightest pillar | That one of truest gold | This transparent loving killer | Of all tales ever told.

All love is unrequited | Of one for the one | An infinitely sided | All-consuming sun.

Cross yourself off of your list | Scratch out my blind I | This is no place for a tryst | Nor kiss or a sigh.

Nobody lives for themselves | That is a huge lie |
Crafted by the little elves | Who see when you'll
die.

A bite with two black dots from | Transylvania |
An eye whose pupil rots from | Monomania.

Just heartsick as usual | Knowing all is well | One
more irresponsible | Self-creating hell.

Now that thought is impossible | I will stay
everywhere | Thanks to the love most horrible |
You sighed into the air.

Was born on the day I died | Will die today born
| Laughing the hours all cried | From night until
morn.

To see where the problem lies | Is that why you
sigh? | Remembering someone's eyes | Not a day
goes by.

The hardest thing in the world | Not to hear from
him | Around whose pure glance is curled | The
core of all whim.

Mistake to think there's someone | In the world at all | And yet we're under this sun | Neither great nor small.

Maybe you don't understand | What became of me | That day the sky and the land | Sank into the sea.

Impossible not to feel | That this is all wrong | That the infinitely real | Is taking too long.

It tricks life into living | With the simplest ruse | A gift that keeps on giving | One nothing to lose.

Long javelins of longing | Launched from every ship | Of the lost fleet belonging | To your smiling lip.

I swim lost in my own eyes | Searching for the day | When eternity's sunrise | Lights our lonely way.

Love the god now appearing | Between us and us | Never mind their mad fearing | The sad human fuss.

That of which reality | Is but one result | And whose actuality | Is the true occult.

I the future of all stars | I the true abyss | I the victor of all wars | I the sovereign bliss.

Heart beating day in day out | The name of a prayer | Mind humming past fear or doubt | A pure helpless care.

And if the time never comes | Today will be it | Eternal now of all hums | Word of every wit.

In tornado of my mind | Feeling for the key | One true word that will unbind | Silence ever free.

As if one needs to be reminded | How impossible we are | As if there is someone not blinded | By the sheer fact of this star.

This is not a good idea | This does not make sense | Only one word do I hear | With no toward or whence.

Hide me in the ancient fold | Long before all birth | Now that life is growing cold | On this marble earth.

Only chance to cross this line | Between I and I | To follow that one way sign | Once before you die.

To evaporate oneself | Like a flowering rose | To open an eye of life | That will never close.

It's all pride and vanity | Thinking you're someone | A supreme insanity | Of not being none.

Everything that you despise | Is within yourself | All the evil, sin, and lies | And in no one else.

If this is the universe | Then where is its place? | If there is anything worse | Then what is its trace?

Abandon yourself faster | Than you can respire | Obey the only master | Of every desire.

To see that you have been lost | Longer than you've been | To flee no matter the cost | All that one is in.

Every time I unawake | From that black abyss | One tiniest sip I take | Of infinite bliss.

Was not and is no longer | Always is never | This strength becoming stronger | Than all forever.

Go to where you are going | Stay right where you stay | Know that which you are knowing | Play the game to play.

A desire more terrible | Than desire itself | A fire more unbearable | Than the fires of hell.

Locate the small part of you | Not ready to die | Pluck its sweet root for the stew | Cooking without why.

Expeller-pressed through the crowd | Of feelings and thoughts | Over-dressed in silence loud | Black hole polka dots.

Point at which one learns to long | In a whole new way | Piercing cosmos with a song | That no one can say.

Only the eternal one | East, west, north, and south | A sole all-consuming sun | Swallowing your mouth.

Kindly stay away from me | Further from yourself | Maybe that way we may see | What lies past this hell.

As if I might offer you | Anything but death | As if the sky's perfect blue | Is not my own breath.

Separate yourself from you | Unstick it from it | Cease to salivate the glue | That becomes your bit.

There is no one in the world | Especially me | All the flags ever unfurled | Not one of them free.

There is no future and no past | Only this one vast thing | One fact that will forever last | Tinier than nothing.

By the noose from which I hang | Sighing in the breeze | Channeling the whimper-bang | Of unending ease.

I, a bundle of sorrow | Slow-burning desire | You, my only tomorrow | Al di là of fire.

Impossible to escape | Having wholly failed | Walking lost in a landscape | Where all views are jailed.

We are fish in the ocean |Swimming to and fro | Drowning slowly in the one | No knowledge will know.

I dedicate myself to | Nothing whatever | Just to escape your untrue | Promise forever.

Ocean is in the ocean | Sky is in the sky | A vast unmoving motion | Without where or why.

To know every dream of you | As unreal as I | Except for the moment true | When we wake and die.

Only one who never fell | Into pits of thought |
Only one not now in hell | Lost in realms of not.

If only I might now see | How insane I am | But,
my dear, hyper-frankly | I don't give a damn.

All greedy for attention | Greediest of all |
Someone no one can mention | Upon whom all
call.

Floating tomb-abyss of love | Gravest cosmic
curse | Without below or above | Only worse and
worse.

Hang me now where I still am | High upon the
tree | Whose roots twist into a dam | Of tears wept
for thee.

Seeing through my own eyelids | Looking round
the room | Finding nothing that forbids | Exiting
the gloom.

The mistake of all lifetimes | Lifetime of mistakes
| Evolution of all slimes | Into total fakes.

Knowing one can do nothing | What is there to do | But observe every being | In light of the true.

Near the center of the earth | Sunk beyond outside | Swimming in the very first | Tear that Satan cried.

Failed in every single way | But that does not stop | A heart from dying to stay | Drowning in each drop.

Happy for the love one felt | Now is time to go | Fuel fire of the final melt | Burn the first real glow.

Perhaps if someone had stopped | Long before time was | Then all the heads ever chopped | Would perceive the cause.

I wish you saw God's dancing | In my dream last night | Highest, happiest prancing | Of heaviest light.

Suffer the hypocrisy | Of being in hell | The split personality | Of your very self.

To stick on yourself every name | While dropping them all | To skip between stones of the same | And never once fall.

Their project is to describe | Their current project | While other designs inscribe | Themselves into act.

Across all universes | One looking for one | Beyond all bests and worses | Blindest blinding sun.

Funny how the silence blabs | Of all things and none | Murdering each thought that stabs | Into its vast sun.

All things ahead of schedule | Except you and you | Not one moment ever dull | Save the two, the two.

No one cares and no one can | Problem is with those | Who pressurize the human | To lie through its nose.

God delete me from the list | Of those off the list | Kiss me back among the kissed | By kisses you kissed.

As soon as your narrative | Now comes crashing down | Shall we meet where none may live | Near center of town?

Seen the men and the women | And some neithers too | Yet nowhere nor anywhen | Anyone like you.

Here is where I take a bow | To my own dead self | Sans whom I'd not be here now | Being dragged through hell.

The way lost so many times | That there is no way | Nothing but the silent chimes | Leading time astray.

As if being owns being | As if it does not | As if a total seeming | Is not all you've got.

Long trail of senseless sorrow | Leading back to here | Future of all tomorrow | Source of every tear.

Maybe not the worst idea | Before dropping coat
| Flying far away from here | To leave a brief note.

Drowning up the mountainside | Climbing down
the sea | Swallowing new ways untried | Between
you and me.

Trap you are in is your trap | Wherefore you are
in | Walking in a roadless map | Of bone, flesh,
and skin.

And now to wait in the tomb | Inhaling these sighs
| Seven thousand years of doom | For each of our
lies.

Now that I have lost the way | Time to lose myself
| Faster than someone might say | Follow me
through hell.

Losing among signs astray | The way and the goal
| Twenty-four hours a day | Dark night of the soul.

That thought itself cannot not | Think always of
you | Must bear gladly as my lot | This fate sad but
true.

Time is shining, space is abuzz | Everything is clear | Universe is smiling because | My love is not here.

One to whom I always turn | Still turning away | Face of fire in which I burn | That will never stay.

Yes it is what it is yes | No not as we say | Better than anyone's guess | In the worst worst way.

No wonder you left at once | Seeing I was there | No one wants to be someone's | Object of despair.

As if anyone is here | Anyone but you | As if anything more near | Will ever be true.

So your feelings are nothing | Your ideas are shit | No worries cause everything | Because this is it.

Art opening of her tomb | All abuzz with death | Dropping honey from the womb | Kissed by the first breath.

I am the mirror walking | All day through your heart | I am the no one stalking | The end and the start.

Say no and keep saying no | Until no is yes | Not of friend and not of foe | One, oppositeless.

Lost in the veils of a face | Reaching for a star | Near the summit of this trace | Of the one you are.

The vertical is within | High above the black | Falling from the ancient chin | Of the head you lack.

Wearing yourself out of you | Rubbing off the sky | Sinking underneath the blue | Falling above why.

All things attend to all things | Playing the whole part | Of one who all alone brings | Forth all with no art.

Fate of thought is suicide | Nothing left to do | For the lonely thing that died | Trying to be you.

To see that all you're made of | Is sorrow and lust | Mixed with a small drop of love | That no one may trust.

For even if you flay me | Straight down to the bone | Take it all and betray me | This fate is my own.

At center of all coldness | On ember I blow | A burning secret boldness | One only will know.

Sometimes a whole universe | Will just walk away | Leave you not better nor worse | With nothing to say.

If knew how to be human | Likely would not be | That's just a nature which can | Pretend to be me.

Desire thinks that not wanting | Will somehow deprive you | Whereas it is the sad haunting | That cannot survive you.

Everyone believes in God | Whatever they say | A subtle look, sigh, or nod | Gives it all away.

No one is really honest | To be them they can't |
Behold the entangled nest | From which grows
this plant.

Death is gonna let you down | Not be what you
want | Here now is the place to drown | This the
only front.

There never was anything | For you in this world
| Nothing except the nothing | All around all
curled.

The world is foaming with souls | Bubbling with
faces | Flowing over its own holes | Drowning in
traces.

People are not very smart | And yet they know
more | Than may be produced by art | Or
destroyed by war.

Made the mistake of talking | After my first word
| Chose the error of walking | Toward a world I
heard.

No wonder I am sorrow | Being only me |
Yesterday to tomorrow | Dead eternally.

Seeing that I want to die | Will go on living | This
life whose death is a lie | Endless beginning.

Infinitely mistaken | Eternally dumb | Absolutely
forsaken |Torturously numb.

No one really loves anyone | And yet love is true |
Existing like a shining sun | Above me and you.

No one knows what's happening | Why we are all
here | Into what life's expanding | Year by year by
year.

Goodbye all and hello none | Welcome to my
world | A limitless room for one | Paradise
unfurled.

No one has made it this far | Neither you nor me
| Sunset is only a star | Not touching the sea.

One kills oneself for breakfast | Eats the corpse
for lunch | Dines on the shadow it cast | And dies
to the munch.

Soul-bee sleeping in the Rose | Dreaming bright flowers | Stung awake by sorrow-throes | Of blinding powers.

See and drop every detail | Of your little life | Just the devil's in that hell | Only war and strife.

You are me so I'm all yours | Please do as you please | I'm tired of fighting love's wars | And weeping its seas.

One of a few people never | Ever to exist | Unborn dead from no life severed | Unwritten off the list.

O how excited I was | Before you were you | O how delighted I was | When nothing was true.

Imagine what it is like | Never to be God | The total length of that spike | The void of that clod.

Funny how pessimism | Gets cosmic so fast | Anything to remain dumb | To the one outcast.

What cowardice to insist | That the world improve | Shaking in its air a fist | Screaming about love.

Gift wrap the whole thing for God | To no one supreme | Signed with the pen of a nod | On paper of dream.

You know how it came this | How it follows you | Across the best worst abyss | Of truth truly true.

A strength of constant breaking | Breathing drowning sigh | The will of one life taking | All of time to die.

Not in this life and not not | Nowhere around here | Somewhere every place forgot | Near far and far near.

Blood sputters where heart is shot | Like it has a choice | Creature cries when it is caught | Finding losing voice.

Everything left to say | Everything to do | Nothing seen along the way | Nothing except you.

To erase all expectations | Without tearing the page | To escape all limitations | Without breaking the cage.

It knows no biography | Voyage outside death | Sailing the geography | Of its very breath.

It records more than it sees | Projects beyond known | Is home to birds, snakes, and bees | This heart overgrown.

Comfort in the only fact | That all is now won | And the sole remaining act | Is to be undone.

To step out of the mirror | Of one's enchantment | To decapitate the sphere | Of self-entrapment.

For sure I am mistaken | Beyond any doubt | Definitely forsaken | Bound by no way out.

Way of life and life of way | Never turning back | Always finding time to stay | For the next attack.

Will die if I don't wake up | If I do I will | Should you take from me this cup | Don't forget to spill.

Leave all alone forever | Go nowhere so fast | That the essence of never | Burns up in the blast.

Love is real and I am not | That is how it goes | In one vast netless net caught | Where the wild wind blows.

I'm stepping over the edge | Far beyond the blue | Only to find one more ledge | Made by you know who.

Yes but what your being right | Says right through your eyes | Is that you so love to fight | And are full of lies.

Lump self spinning on time's lathe | Soon to be a sphere | Or whatever perfect shape | They make around here.

The only friend is the friend | We are his shadows | Puppet-forms whose strings' end | No one ever knows.

No one is available | To answer your call | Yes put me through ASAP | For she is my all.

Once to see what I have seen | Is to never be | So blind I'll stay to that scene | By just being me.

There is not much to see here | And yet more than all | None only one to be here | On this little ball.

If thinking is a hole | Thought something dead | Then my heart is a bowl | Shot in the head.

Yes of course this is the worst | And that is the best | No way else for the accursed | To ever find rest.

Insane yes that's accurate | Not perfect but good | True but gives too much credit | To this bleached driftwood.

No one knows their great fortune | To be here right now | Hearing God's holy organ | So howlessly howl.

So tell me how it would work | If this life were real | After impossible birth | Before death's plain seal.

You in your life and I in mine | Now isn't that most odd? | Don't worry if there isn't time | Just be quiet and nod.

Opening ( )hole in my head | Taking several years | Operation void with lead | So I'm using tears.

It's absolutely great how | Anything at all | And absolutely sad now | That it's all so small.

Outright humiliation | Erasure of stance | Incessant conflagration | Death's own dying dance.

If only I had not sighed | Only no one spoke | If only nobody died | Only nothing broke.

There is no one to talk to | And nothing to say | No where or when to walk to | And better that way?

One tongue at least talking sense | On caravan Earth | Music almost too intense | For those born by birth.

Too infinite the dead end | Too vast the un-place
| Too perfect the only friend | Too absent the face.

Silence suffering silence | Ear screaming shut
mouth | Impenetrable violence | No way in or out.

Fate is fate — the rest is not | Just the unfolding |
Of a flower no one ought | To be found holding.

The presence of a question | That won't go away |
A stopping at the station | That will never stay.

The last thing happiness needs | For you to be it |
And first of its seeds | Overgrowing wit.

Cut the knife out of my heart | Before it kills all |
Or leave it as per your art | It is not my call.

In hell and that is OK | Not to worry about | All
signs show this is the way | The only way out.

Pretty sure I never lived | Certain I am dead | That
this whole life was born hid | In a severed head.

Person who you think you are | Is a pure fiction |
The mask sounding near and far | A ghostly
diction.

To whom else am I to talk? | The world is desert |
No one nowhere on a walk | Stirring up the dirt.

Is it all just one huge fraud | Big lie of desire? |
NO screams the soul's lighting rod | Flame is sign
of fire.

Just scream NO and all is well | Silently of course
| No one needs the yet worse hell | Of your going
hoarse.

A dead man has no business | Thinking suicide |
Worrying over abyss | Or counting tears cried.

In the middle of this this | Too long silent fight |
Mirror unmirroring bliss | Shadowfullest light.

If this love you cannot see | What more can I say?
| Essence of evil is we | The worst thing today.

I don't want to see my face | Ever hear my thoughts | I hope every single trace | Of this thick veil rots.

A sub-calendar of days | Spiraling far down | Sigh-following all the ways | Into which we drown.

Wasted life and wasted death | Wasted words and deeds | Wasted thought and wasted breath | Wasted wants and needs.

One who shows me where I am | Nowhere to be found | And yet the little lost lamb | Is still on the ground.

Being led through every maze | Every twist and turn | Until lostness's own ways | Stop, listen, and learn.

When everything disappears | Then it is all there | Abyss back into you peers | And it is not air.

Observe who talks about whom | Therewith draw the line | Between healthy, natural bloom | And a moldy vine.

As if there is something else | Anymore than this | Or less than such perfect hells | Made by the one bliss.

Of course there is no friend, friend | Perforce no one there | Apart from pure love's one end | There is just despair.

Wanted there to be someone | And of course there's not | Nor no one under the sun | In life's mirror caught.

All mistakes made corrected | By future mistakes | All crimes performed detected | By comic outtakes.

As truth finally sinks in | And the deal is done | Take forever to drink in | All you never won.

Lonely with the only one | All-where to be seen | Nowhere far-near the sole sun | That has always been.

Unless you stay where you are | Unless burrow in | Unless gravitate a star |

And still talking to no one | After all this time |
And still walking where the fun | Is misspilled in
rhyme.

To lie as one in the tomb | All day and all night |
To know there alone is room | For darkness and
light.

In the wasteland of my sighs | There is still
perfume | Formed like moonlight in the eyes |
Thinking of your tomb.

The maze is only the maze | Neither lost nor not |
Simply the ways of its ways | Knot a string forgot.

You the being of my being | Heaviest of lead |
Lightest light of all seeing | Head without a head.

Expected my existence | To be acknowledged |
The stupidest insistence | On a falsest pledge.

Yes you must go much deeper | Far deeper than
deep | To dance above the reaper | Yourself
overleap.

One hundred one percent death | Life no turning back | Never recovering breath | Retreating attack.

Never trust a human being | But only the one | Whose darkest deception seen | Is the earth's own sun.

Thank God I do not exist | How else to take it? | Only never on the list | Will ever make it.

The bliss transforms to nightmare | Back again to bliss | Until there's no one to care | What becomes of this.

If love is deepest fire | Penetrating bone | I am coldest desire | Paralyzing stone.

Tear the heart out through my eyes | Tie it in your hair | Hang all in the secret skies | Where our one is there.

Since I am not here at all | And all life is dead | There's zero to climb or fall | Neither foot nor head.

( )ntegrate into silence | Leave this noise behind |
The sole existent violence | Of my own sick mind.

Fading deep into the new | Far beyond the grave
| Within the eyes seeing through | No one left to
save.

Maybe tomorrow I will | Or rather will not | Now
that there's no time until | Time all time forgot.

Moved my lips speaking your name | And they
were not there | Being burned off in the plane |
Crashing everywhere.

Life and death walk before me | As I lag behind |
Navigating the stormy |Seas of no one's mind.

Hanging in the silver sky | Breathing through a
thread | Waiting for the sun to die | Deep inside
my head.

No more tell you dreams as these | No one cares
to hear | New secrets from a lost breeze | Stirring
in my ear.

Since nothing removes this pain | It must nothing be | Nothing but a drop of rain | Between I and me.

Angel in a heart of tears | Mirroring the one | Whose face so ancient of years | Lights the newest sun.

For years losing only way | Three times each second | Too many zeroes to say | Once upon an end.

This here dead end now landed in | Vaster than universe | Not bad spot to be stranded in | Since it's gonna get worse.

Can't stand being anything | Nor knower nor known | A wound poisoning the sting | This life none my own.

No one sees where we all are | Whither to and fro | Whence led by the only star | With nowhere to go.

How a Knot Became the Rope | By Never-Born
Died | Lost, stuck, and losing all hope | Was
somehow untied.

The wound swallowing all wounds | Sorrow of
sorrows | The doom saving all the doomed | From
their tomorrows.

If this here world were our home | We would not
be here | But outside somewhere to roam | And
play without fear.

Reality likes to be | Both you and not you |
Seeking something left to see | Something right to
do.

Locked everything up inside | Til I was there too
| Tower wherein someone died | Remembering
you.

Only way is not to want | Otherwise it's death |
Far worse than the one that haunts | Every living
breath.

All day and night you listen | Lacking else to do |
To your own thought's sad lesson | While it
laughs at you.

True that I'm totally lost | No clue what to do |
Better than becoming ghost | Or room with no
view.

For years thought I was flying | Falling yet lower
| To ground where I am lying | Grave of the
knower.

Seeing that somewhere is hell | Is just another
way | Of knowing all shall be well | In paradise
today.

As there is nothing to say | Will goes on trying |
Suddenly to birth someday | A word undying.

gnOme is a secret press specializing in the publication of anonymous, pseudepigraphical, and apocryphal works from the past, present, and future.

"Open my grave after my death and see how / The smoke of the fire within me rises from my shroud" (Hafiz)

gnOme is acephalic.

GNOMEBOOKS.WORDPRESS.COM